ON THE EDGE
AGAINST THE ODDS

Henry Billings
Melissa Billings

Series Editor: Amy Collins
Executive Editor: Linda Kwil
Production Manager: Genevieve Kelley
Marketing Manager: Sean Klunder
Cover Design: Michael E. Kelly

McGraw-Hill Contemporary

Send all inquiries to:
McGraw-Hill/Contemporary
130 East Randolph Street, Suite 400
Chicago, Illinois 60601

ISBN: 0-07-285197-X

Printed in the United States of America.

1 2 3 4 5 6 7 8 9 10 QPD 08 07 06 05 04 03

To the Student iv

How to Use This Book v

UNIT 1 **TRAPPED!**

   SELECTION 1 Trapped in a Cave 1

   SELECTION 2 Buried Under a Mosque 4

UNIT 2 **LOST PEOPLE**

   SELECTION 1 A Doctor Ducks Out 12

   SELECTION 2 "Like a Grain of Rice" 16

UNIT 3 **MEDICAL MIRACLES**

   SELECTION 1 Shark Attack 24

   SELECTION 2 A Hole in His Head 28

UNIT 4 **WHAT A WAY TO GO**

   SELECTION 1 No One Noticed 36

   SELECTION 2 Strange Tales of Death 40

UNIT 5 **INTO THE JUNGLE**

   SELECTION 1 Amazon Nightmare 48

   SELECTION 2 "They're Killing Us!" 52

UNIT 6 **THAT'S GOTTA HURT!**

   SELECTION 1 Look Out Below! 60

   SELECTION 2 No Walk in the Park 64

UNIT 7 **SEA TALES**

   SELECTION 1 Survival on a Desert Island 72

   SELECTION 2 Clinging to Life 76

UNIT 8 **ON FIRE**

   SELECTION 1 In Over Their Heads 84

   SELECTION 2 Townhouse Tragedy 88

UNIT 9 **WATER, WATER EVERYWHERE**

   SELECTION 1 Miracle in a Tree 96

   SELECTION 2 Tragic Mudslide 100

UNIT 10 **THE STRONG SURVIVE**

   SELECTION 1 Icicle Baby 108

   SELECTION 2 No Way Out 112

Words-per-Minute Table 120

Plotting Your Progress: Reading Speed 121

Photo Credits 122

SAMPLE LESSON

To the Student

The average person would not survive being stranded on a desert island or a plane crash in the jungle. Most people would not survive jumping from an airplane without a working parachute. *On the Edge: Against the Odds* is a collection of stories about people who live despite impossible odds. A castaway survives on the ocean for 14 days in a dinghy with nothing but a fishing pole. A woman who is nine months pregnant is stranded in a tree during southern Africa's worst flooding in 100 years. After an accident, nine miners survive 240 feet below ground for 73 hours. An eight-year-old boy is attacked by a shark off the coast of Florida. An iron rod shoots through the head of a railroad worker. Would you be strong enough to survive?

As you read the stories in this book, you will be developing your reading skills. The lessons will help you increase your reading speed while you improve your reading comprehension, critical thinking skills, and vocabulary. Many of the exercises are similar to questions you will see on state and national tests. Learning how to complete them will help you prepare for tests you will take in the future. Some of the exercises encourage you to write sentence or paragraph responses. As you write your opinions, you will learn to support them with specific examples from the stories you read.

You never know how you might react in a dangerous situation. You hope you will be strong enough to survive. One thing is for certain: you won't be able to take your eyes off each page until you've read the book cover to cover.

How to Use This Book

ABOUT THE BOOK *On the Edge: Against the Odds* has ten units, each of which contains two stories and a lesson. The stories are about people who have survived through medical miracles and tales of adventure gone badly wrong. Each story is followed by a page of reading comprehension exercises. These exercises will help you to better understand the article. At the end of each unit are exercises that help develop vocabulary and critical thinking skills. These exercises will assist your understanding of the similarities between the two stories and will help relate them to your own experiences.

THE SAMPLE LESSON The first lesson in the book is a sample that demonstrates how the units are organized. The sample lesson will show you how to complete the exercises. The correct answers to the questions are included.

WORKING THROUGH EACH UNIT Begin each unit by looking at the photograph. Before you begin reading, think about your reaction to the photo and predict what you think the article might be about. Then read the article.

Sometimes you or your teacher may want to time how long it takes you to read a story. You can write your time in the circle at the end of each story. Use the Words-per-Minute Table on page 120 to find your reading speed and record it on the Plotting Your Progress graph on page 121. As you read through the book, you will be able to watch your reading speed improve on the graph.

After you read the article and record your speed, begin the exercises. The comprehension section will test your understanding of what you have read. The vocabulary exercises will include words that were used in both stories. The critical thinking exercises will help you build analytical skills. Some of the exercises will ask you to write a paragraph giving your thoughts and opinions about the stories. Answers to all the exercises can be found in the *On the Edge Teacher's Guide.*

Trapped in a Cave

It started out as a test. Seven Swiss students wanted to challenge themselves. They wanted to see how well they could work together. So they set off to explore an underground cave in Goumois, France. The students, who were all in their twenties, didn't have any experience as spelunkers. The teacher who went with them didn't either. Still, it seemed like a reasonable adventure. Lots of beginners went spelunking in this cave. The cave had long, winding passageways that were fun to explore. The cave was not very deep, so it didn't seem dangerous. On Wednesday, May 16, 2001, however, this seemingly safe cave became a death-trap.

It was late in the afternoon when the three women and five men entered the cave. As they explored inside, it started to rain. The rain created a raging current of water that swept through the cave. The students and their teacher had no time to get out. They were trapped by the flash flood. With the water level rising all around them, they could only scramble onto a ledge and hope the water would not reach them.

Meanwhile, school officials grew worried. Time passed, and yet the students and their teacher didn't come back. Around midnight, the school declared them missing. French rescue workers rushed to the cave. So did Swiss rescue workers. In all, about 300 people came to help. Some brought diving equipment. They planned to swim through the flooded cave in search of the stranded explorers. But the water was too high and the current too strong for them to make it through the cave's narrow entrance.

On Thursday morning, rescuers set up pumps. They began pumping water away from the cave entrance. They managed to lower the water level two and a half feet. But then heavy rain came again. The rain pushed the water level back up. It remained impossible for anyone to get into the cave.

As the hours slipped by, rescuers grew increasingly worried. The odds of finding the spelunkers alive were getting smaller.

"The only chance for survival is if the group managed to get to a place with an air pocket," said Thomas Abenz of the Swiss Society for Cave Research.

There were a couple of big chambers in the cave. If the group had reached one of these, they might have found an air pocket. They might still be alive. But there were no guarantees. Even if the water was only waist deep, the students wouldn't last long. The water was so cold that they would soon freeze to death.

By Thursday night, rescuers were feeling desperate. They brought in some explosives and blew a wider hole at the entrance of the cave. At last divers could go in. Working in shifts, they began to search the mile-long cave and its many side passages. But as the night wore on, hope faded. None of the divers saw any sign of the missing spelunkers.

On Friday morning, rescuers drilled down into one of the known air chambers in the cave. They hoped the group of eight had taken refuge there. Hopes rose a bit as the drilling went on. But when the chamber was opened, it was empty.

As a last-ditch effort, divers went into the cave one more time. When they came out, they brought great news. They had found all eight spelunkers in a chamber with an air pocket. They were on a dry ledge about eighty yards from the entrance. All of them were alive.

The passageway leading to the chamber contained a lot of water. But rescuers thought the spelunkers could walk out with their heads just above water. Two French divers went in to guide them out. But before they could do so, the sky opened and rain poured down. Again the underground cave was filled with a dark, swirling river. The flooding was so intense that even the two French divers couldn't get out.

"Everyone is astounded, even the specialists, about where the water is coming from," said one official.

Rescuers tried to work the pumps to open the entrance again. But there was simply too much water. And the current remained too strong for other divers to risk going in. All through the night, rescuers waited for conditions to improve.

At last, on Saturday morning, the rain abated. The pumps began to work again. Rescuers also used dynamite to blow open new sections of the cave. This helped drain more water out.

Once again, divers plunged into the cave. They took ropes and pulleys with them. This time they got lucky. The rain held off. A couple of hours later, they brought the three women out of the cave. All three were cold, tired, and hungry. They were covered with mud. But they were alive. Rescuers cheered when they emerged.

Next the men were brought out. They, too, were exhausted. They were stumbling. Some were in tears. But even as they cried, they were smiling. "Thank you for the help," one of them said to the crowd of rescuers. "Thank you for everything."

Everyone was thrilled by the success of the rescue mission. And everyone wholeheartedly agreed when the director of the school declared, "I'm so happy this nightmare is over!"

When you finish reading, subtract your start time from your end time. This is how long it took you to read the selection. Enter your reading time below.

If you have been timed while reading this article, enter your reading time below. Then turn to the Words-per-Minute Table on page 120 and look up your reading speed (words per minute). Enter your reading speed on the graph on page 121.

Reading Time: Selection 1

_____ : _____
MINUTES   SECONDS

Work through the exercises on this page.
If necessary, refer back to the story.

UNDERSTANDING IDEAS Circle the letter of the best answer.

1. The Swiss students were trapped in the cave because

A a large rock fell and blocked their way

(B) *water from a rainstorm flooded the cave*

C they went in too far and became lost

D the batteries in their flashlights ran out

2. Which statement belongs in the empty box?

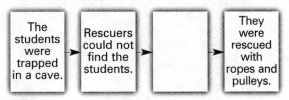

The students were trapped in a cave. → Rescuers could not find the students. → [ ] → They were rescued with ropes and pulleys.

(F) *Divers got trapped with the students.*

G Everyone cheered when the students came out of the cave.

H Officials reported the students were missing.

J The students thanked the rescuers for saving their lives.

3. After the divers were trapped with the students, officials

A thought the rescue effort had failed

B told new divers they must go into the cave right away

C waited a week before starting to work again

(D) *wondered where the water was coming from*

4. The reader can conclude that the rescuers

(F) *would not give up*

G did not try very hard

H did not have the right equipment

J were sure they would find the students

SUMMARIZE For each blank, choose the word that best completes the meaning of the paragraph.

| stranded | located | |
| explore | ledge | current |

On May 16, 2001, seven students and a teacher set off to _____*explore*_____ an underground cave. After they entered the cave, it began to rain. A powerful _____*current*_____ of water trapped them inside the cave. Fortunately, they found a _____*ledge*_____ above the water where they were safe. Rescue divers tried to swim into the cave to find the _____*stranded*_____ students. At last, the divers _____*located*_____ the students and brought them out to safety.

IF YOU WERE THERE Write a brief paragraph explaining what you might do if you were trapped with the students. Be sure to include examples from the story to support your response.

Like the students, I would look for the highest ledge in the

cave. Then I would make sure we all stayed together.

I would try not to get discouraged and to hope rescuers

arrived soon!

_____

Read the next article and complete the exercises that follow.

3

Buried Under a Mosque

The rain came down in torrents. But that didn't stop people from going to the 2:00 P.M. prayer service at the Karounwi Central Mosque. Dozens of people showed up for this mid-afternoon call to prayer on April 18, 2001. They weren't the only ones in the two-story building. Many children attended the Muslim Junior School there. And a few people had ducked into the mosque just to get out of the rain. So in all, there were close to seventy people in the building when disaster struck.

The prayer service didn't last long. By 2:10, it was over. Some people had already gone back out into the wet streets of Lagos, Nigeria. Others were getting ready to leave. Suddenly there came a loud crack.

"We thought it was thunder," said ten-year-old Taiye Olawuwo.

Others thought the same thing. And perhaps there *was* a clap of thunder just at that moment. But there was another sound as well—the sound of the mosque walls collapsing. In the space of a few seconds, the entire building crumbled.

"I heard the building creaking and I jumped out," said Wasiu Salihu. He was one of the lucky ones. Most did not have time to react. A man who worked nearby said the building "came down like a pack of cards."

"The whole roof caved in immediately," agreed someone else.

Eleven-year-old Ibrahim was inside the mosque when it fell. "We just heard a big noise and before we knew it, everywhere was dark," he said.

On the street outside, people stared in horror. Many screamed and sobbed. They began to claw at the rubble with their bare hands, hoping to reach those trapped inside. Some ran to their homes and brought back bowls or pans. They used these to scoop away bits of dirt, stone, and metal. Soon rescue crews showed up. They brought shovels. A bulldozer came. A construction company sent a crane to help move the bigger pieces of concrete. Even street gangs rallied to help. These gangs often caused trouble. But on this day, they did what they could to aid the rescue effort. Some of the victims managed to crawl out. Others were pulled out.

As young Ibrahim lay in the darkness, he saw a small opening. "I was able to push away a fairly big stone covering the space," he said. "Then I put my hand through the space for people to see me. . . . I just shouted for them to hear me."

Rescue workers did hear Ibrahim. They pulled him to safety. He was not hurt. But many others who had been inside the mosque were injured or even killed. At one point, rescue workers came upon a pair of hands sticking up through the wreckage. The hands were clasped as though in prayer. But there was no life left in them.

All afternoon and into the night, rescue workers kept working. They could hear the voices of those still buried in the debris.

"There are three children and two other bodies under the wreckage, while some more people are crying for help," one person reported.

"I can see three other bodies," called another.

"I think there are many more buried in there," another said sadly.

Around 9:00 P.M., rescue crews reached Risikatu Summonu. This 82-year-old woman was well known to all. She sold bean cakes in the neighborhood. She was alive when workers found her. But she was badly hurt. An ambulance rushed her to the hospital. But she died before getting there.

By morning, rescue crews were losing hope. They did not think they would find any more survivors.

"In view of the heat and suffocation, it will be very difficult for anybody to survive after twenty-four hours," one doctor said.

Indeed, no one was found alive that day—or the next, or the next. As people mourned the loss of life, they started to ask questions. They wanted to know why the mosque had collapsed. Some thought lightning was to blame. Others believed it was the heavy rain. Some pointed out that the top floor of the mosque had just been built. They thought the walls were too weak to support the extra weight. Still others saw the tragedy as fate. As one man said, "It is an act of God and nobody can say exactly what happened since it was destined to happen."

On April 19, two thousand people came to the site of the disaster. They came to watch the rescue and pray. They also came to reflect on what had happened. For some, it had been a close call. For those who had lost loved ones, however, life would never be the same. They would remember April 18, 2001, as a day when part of their world collapsed.

If you have been timed while reading this article, enter your reading time below. Then turn to the Words-per-Minute Table on page 120 and look up your reading speed (words per minute). Enter your reading speed on the graph on page 121.

Reading Time: Selection 2

_____ : _____
MINUTES   SECONDS

UNDERSTANDING IDEAS Circle the letter of the best answer.

1. **When people heard a loud crack, it was the sound of**

   A the walls of the mosque collapsing

   B a thunderstorm

   C a large stone falling from the roof of a nearby building

   D a construction crane that had fallen over

2. **A doctor said it would be difficult to survive more than 24 hours because**

   F it was going to rain some more

   G the rescuers had given up quickly

   H of heat and suffocation

   J the rescuers could not work at night

3. **What is the most likely reason street gangs were willing to help the rescuers?**

   A The police forced them to help.

   B They were always helping out in the area.

   C Even they realized that many people were hurt or dying.

   D Someone offered to pay them money.

4. **According to the article**

   F everyone knew why the mosque had collapsed

   G an explosion caused the collapse

   H someone intentionally caused the collapse

   J there were several possible reasons why the mosque collapsed

SUMMARIZE For each blank, choose the word that best completes the meaning of the paragraph.

raining	reflect	prayer
rubble	rescued	building

On April 18, 2001, about seventy people gathered for the 2 P.M. _____ service at a mosque in Lagos, Nigeria. That day it had been _____ heavily. Suddenly, with a loud noise, the _____ crumbled to the ground. Many people were trapped under the _____. Some people were _____, but many were badly hurt or killed. Two days later, two thousand people came to pray and _____ on what had happened.

IF YOU WERE THERE Write a brief paragraph explaining what you would have done if you had seen the mosque collapse. Be sure to include examples from the story to support your response.

_____

_____

_____

_____

_____

USE CONTEXT CLUES When you read, you may find a word whose meaning is unfamiliar to you. When that happens, you can look up the word's meaning in the dictionary. You can also find out what the word means by looking for context clues. These are words or sentences that come before or after the word. Context clues can be synonyms or antonyms of the unfamiliar word. They may also be an example or definition of the unfamiliar word.

Read each excerpt from the stories you just read. Circle the letter with the best meaning of the underlined word.

1. **The rain created a <u>raging</u> current of water that swept through the cave. . . . They were trapped by the flash flood.**

   A slow

   B gentle

   C wild

   D soft

2. **With the water level rising all around them, they could only <u>scramble</u> onto a ledge and hope the water would not reach them.**

   F walk

   G climb quickly

   H skip

   J fall slowly

3. **And perhaps there *was* a <u>clap</u> of thunder just at that moment. But there was another sound as well—the sound of the mosque walls collapsing.**

   A blow

   B applause

   C loud sound

   D shot

4. **At one point, rescue workers came upon a pair of hands sticking up through the wreckage. . . . Workers could hear the voices of those still buried in the <u>debris</u>.**

   F street, highway

   G water

   H sand

   J ruins, rubble

5. **As people mourned the loss of life, they started asking questions. They wanted to know why the mosque had <u>collapsed</u>.**

   A fallen apart

   B grown

   C burned

   D been repaired

PUT WORDS INTO CONTEXT Complete the paragraph using the underlined words from the exercise on this page.

Before the disaster at the mosque in Nigeria, there

had been a _____ rainstorm.

After the building _____,

many people were trapped. Rescue workers searched for

survivors in the _____.

Some lucky people had been able to

_____ to safety; others had not.

Some of the survivors said they had heard a loud

_____ of thunder just before the

building fell.

ANTONYMS An antonym is a word that has the opposite meaning of another word. For example, *remember* is an antonym for the word *forget*.

Circle the letter of the word or phrase that means the OPPOSITE of the underlined word.

1. **It was late afternoon when three women and five men <u>entered</u> the cave.**
   - A left
   - B went into
   - C lit
   - D washed

2. **Meanwhile, school officials grew <u>worried</u>.**
   - F anxious, nervous
   - G sad
   - H excited
   - J content, calm

3. **All through the night, rescuers waited for conditions to <u>improve</u>.**
   - A rise
   - B get better
   - C worsen
   - D remain the same

4. **"The whole roof caved in <u>immediately</u>," agreed someone else.**
   - F right away
   - G later
   - H quickly
   - J softly

5. **They did not think that they would find any more <u>survivors</u>.**
   - A adults
   - B victims
   - C rescuers
   - D children

ANTONYM ANALOGIES Analogies show similar patterns between words. Antonym analogies show patterns between words that have opposite meanings. For example, *large* is to *small* as *tall* is to *short*. For each blank, choose an underlined word from the exercise on this page to correctly complete the analogy.

1. *Dying* is to *living* as *victims* is to

   _____ .

2. *Tall* is to *short* as *exited* is to

   _____ .

3. *Tomorrow* is to *now* as *later* is to

   _____ .

4. *Up* is to *down* as *relaxed* is to

   _____ .

5. *Worse* is to *better* as *decline* is to

   _____ .

ORGANIZE THE FACTS There are several different ways to organize your writing. In stories like the ones you just read, the sequence, or order, of the events is very important. In the charts on this page, fill in events in the order that they happened.

"Trapped in a Cave"
1. On May 16, 2001, seven students and a teacher went spelunking in a cave in France.
2.
3. Divers swam through the cave but could not find the students.
4. The divers located the students, but another storm trapped the divers inside the cave as well.
5. After three days, the rain stopped and everyone was rescued.

"Buried Under a Mosque"
1. On April 18, 2001, a mosque collapsed on top of about seventy people.
2.
3.
4.
5.

PUT DETAILS IN SEQUENCE Choose the best answer for each question.

1. **When did the following happen? Where should it be in the sequence chart "Trapped in a Cave"?**

   > And everyone wholeheartedly agreed when the director of the school declared, "I'm so happy this nightmare is over."

   A after 5

   B between 1 and 2

   C between 2 and 3

   D between 4 and 5

2. **Where should the following be in the sequence chart "Buried Under a Mosque"?**

   > "I heard the building creaking and I jumped out," said Wasiu Salihu.

   F at the beginning of the chart

   G in the middle of the chart

   H toward the end of the chart

   J nowhere on the chart

DRAW CONCLUSIONS A conclusion is a judgment based on information you know. You draw a conclusion by thinking about what you've read and then seeing if you can make a judgment, or general statement, about it. Read this paragraph about being trapped in a coal mine. Then choose the best answer to each question.

[1] Coal miners work far underneath the ground. [2] They often develop breathing problems because of the coal dust. [3] Sometimes there are explosions in the mines, and part of the tunnels may collapse. [4] When this happens, miners may be trapped deep inside the mine. [5] Some rescues have taken many days, and still the miners have survived.

1. **Which conclusion can you draw based on the paragraph above?**

   A Coal miners do not work very hard.

   B Coal mining can be a dangerous job.

   C It is not possible to rescue coal miners after an explosion.

   D The tunnels in a coal mine never collapse.

2. **Which sentence helps you conclude that coal miners may be able to survive an underground explosion?**

   F Sentence 1

   G Sentence 2

   H Sentence 4

   J Sentence 5

3. **Which sentence helps you conclude that coal mining may cause lung problems?**

   A Sentence 1

   B Sentence 2

   C Sentence 3

   D Sentence 5

JUDGE THE EVIDENCE When you make a conclusion, you must judge if the information presented is accurate or convincing. Choose the best answer.

1. **Which statement supports the conclusion that rescuers were losing hope of finding the students?**

   A As a last-ditch effort, divers went into the cave one more time.

   B They hoped the group of eight had taken refuge in an air pocket.

   C They began pumping water away from the cave entrance.

   D The passageway leading to the chamber contained a lot of water.

2. **Which statement supports the conclusion that new construction caused the mosque to collapse?**

   F Some believed it was the heavy rain.

   G The walls were too weak to support the extra weight.

   H People began to ask questions.

   J "I think there are many more buried in there," another said sadly.

YOUR OWN CONCLUSION Pretend that you are someone who is investigating the collapse of the mosque in Nigeria. You must decide what happened and why. State your conclusion and support it with examples from the story.

_____

_____

_____

_____

_____

LOST PEOPLE

A Doctor Ducks Out

Matthew Choyce left without saying goodbye. He slipped out of bed in the middle of the night without waking his wife, Jane Noble. He just grabbed his car keys, went out to his car, and drove off. He never came back.

Both Matthew and Jane were doctors in Newcastle, England. They had been married for two years when Matthew disappeared on October 7, 1997. Until the day he left, they seemed like a happy and successful couple. Jane was expecting a baby, and they were both excited about that.

The night before Matthew left, the couple went to sleep as usual. When Jane woke up a little after midnight and went to the bathroom, Matthew was sleeping peacefully. But when she woke up again at 7:15 A.M., Matthew was gone.

"I rushed to the window to check whether his car was there," Jane said, "but it wasn't."

Jane called her neighbors. Matthew wasn't with them. She called the nearby golf courses. Matthew wasn't there. Finally Jane called the police.

Later that day, the police found Matthew's car six miles from home. It was parked along a road by the ocean. On the front seat was a note. "Dear Jane," it read. "I love you very much. I'm sorry for any trouble. Thank you and my family and friends for all their help and advice." The note was in Matthew's handwriting.

Jane feared it was a suicide letter, but police disagreed. There was something odd about it. It didn't read like most suicide notes. Still, police called in divers to search the area. They found nothing. Meanwhile, Jane went around Newcastle, showing pictures of Matthew. No one remembered seeing him.

Four days passed. During that time, Jane clung to the hope that Matthew would be found alive and well. Then police found his T-shirt. It had washed up on shore near his car. Jane fell apart. To her, this was evidence that Matthew had drowned in the sea.

Again, however, the police had different ideas. Forensics experts pointed out that the shirt was in good condition. It wasn't ripped or torn. They didn't think there was any way it could have washed off a dead body. They thought Matthew had faked a suicide. They suspected he had run off and started a new life, leaving Jane—and everyone else he knew—behind.

Without proof, of course, they couldn't be sure. They would have to wait and see. Jane told a reporter, "The police said that if he had drowned, his body would come back into the bay area within a week, or if it had been swept out to sea it would come back within three weeks further down the coast."

Jane waited a week. She waited three weeks. There was no sign of Matthew's body. She kept waiting, but no body ever washed ashore. She showed Matthew's picture in every homeless shelter for miles around, but no one remembered seeing him. Over the next few months, police received 90 calls from people who thought they had seen Matthew. None of these tips panned out.

At last Jane was forced to deal with the likelihood that Matthew had run off. According to the NMPH, he fit the profile. Men are twice as likely to go missing as women. It happens most often with men between the ages of twenty-six and thirty-five. Matthew Choyce was thirty-four.

Still, Jane had trouble imagining Matthew doing such a thing. She scoured her memory for signs of trouble in the weeks before he disappeared. She remembered that he seemed quiet during his last evening with her. "He didn't want to talk about anything," she recalled. "He'd been like that on and off for three weeks. . . . When I asked what was wrong, he said he was worried about work." Jane believed he liked his work in a hospital emergency department. But he was applying for some consultant jobs, and that was stressful. Was that enough to make him leave his wife and unborn child? It was hard to believe. But what else could Jane conclude?

In June of 1998, Jane gave birth to a son, Iain. A week later, she met with reporters. She let them take pictures of her and Iain. She hoped the pictures might spur Matthew to return. "I just want Matthew to get in touch," she told reporters, "to let him know how I am, how beautiful our baby is, to find out how he is and hug us closely. We really are a family now."

Jane's appeal did not bring any word from Matthew. But Jane was convinced he was out there somewhere. "There's no body," she pointed out. "The T-shirt wasn't damaged, there are the sightings, and I had silent messages left on the answering machine weeks after he went missing, which I'm pretty sure were from Matthew. I'm convinced that given time he'll come back, or I'll find him." She added, "I'm never going to stop looking for him."

That's what Jane said in 1998. But by 2001, she was worn out. She needed a change of scenery. She decided to take Iain and move to Australia. It didn't mean she had given up on Matthew. "Matthew is my husband," she said just before she left, "and whether he's here or not, I still feel married to him." But it did mean that she wasn't expecting him to come home any time soon.

If you have been timed while reading this article, enter your reading time below. Then turn to the Words-per-Minute Table on page 120 and look up your reading speed (words per minute). Enter your reading speed on the graph on page 121.

Reading Time: Selection 1

_____ : _____
MINUTES   SECONDS

UNDERSTANDING IDEAS Circle the letter of the best answer.

1. **Which statement belongs in the empty box?**

When Jane woke up, Matthew was gone. → Police found Matthew's car six miles from home. → [ ] → The police thought Matthew had faked suicide.

   A Matthew was sleeping peacefully.
   B Jane gave birth to their son.
   C The police found Matthew's T-shirt.
   D Jane decided to move to Australia.

2. **Which statement best tells what the police said would happen to Matthew's body if he had drowned?**
   F His body would come back to shore within one to three weeks.
   G His body would never be found.
   H His body would be easily found within a day.
   J His body would come back to shore after one to three months.

3. **Which is the most convincing evidence that Matthew Choyce faked a suicide?**
   A Matthew was applying for some consulting jobs.
   B No one in the homeless shelters had seen Matthew.
   C Jane had reporters take pictures of Iain and her.
   D They never found his body.

4. **Jane probably moved to Australia because**
   F Matthew was thirty-four years old
   G she thought she would find Matthew in Australia
   H she had a new job there that she wanted
   J she wanted to stop thinking about Matthew

SUMMARIZE For each blank, choose the word that best completes the meaning of the paragraph.

miles	disappeared	found
drowned	move	suicide

On October 7, 1997, Matthew Choyce

_____. He left a note in his car, which

was parked six _____ from home. His

wife thought he had committed _____,

but the police were not so sure. They said that if he had

_____, his body would wash up in the

bay or down the coast within a few weeks. But the police

never _____ his body. Three years

later, Jane had still not heard from Matthew and decided

to _____ to Australia.

IF YOU WERE THERE Write a brief paragraph explaining what you would do if you were one of Matthew Choyce's close friends. Be sure to include examples from the story to support your response.

_____

_____

_____

_____

_____

"Like a Grain of Rice"

Everyone loved Jay Carsey. As president of Charles County Community College in Maryland, he had a very high profile. He and his wife Nancy often went to parties and helped with local charity work. They were smart, charming, and gracious to everyone. "We were Mr. and Mrs. Wonderful," said Nancy. But on May 19, 1982, "Mr. Wonderful" turned into "Mr. Weird." He told Nancy that he'd probably be home for lunch. Then he drove to the airport and caught a plane out of town, never to return.

When Jay didn't show up at the office, his secretary grew worried. When he didn't return home that evening, Nancy, too, became alarmed. By the next morning she was hysterical. She thought of all the bad things that could have happened to him. He might have been in a car accident. He might have been kidnapped. But that day's mail brought news she never expected: he had left of his own accord.

The note she got that day was signed simply "J," but she could tell he had written it. It said, "I'm leaving now because I know you can't. I am a physical and psychological disaster. I have no will to improve, and I don't want to drag you down with me."

Nancy was stunned. She had been married to Jay for seventeen years. She hadn't been unhappy and she didn't think he had been, either. She couldn't imagine why he would do something like this. As she said, "I was absolutely shocked and devastated. It didn't seem real. It didn't seem like it really could have happened and I couldn't believe it was happening." She added, "It was like a nightmare that didn't stop."

Wanting to know where Jay had gone and why, Nancy tried to track his moves. At first he had used credit cards, so he had left a trail. He had withdrawn $30,000 in cash from a secret bank account he had kept. Then he had flown to Houston, Texas. He had spent the night in a fancy hotel, and then had flown to San Diego. But there the trail died. He had stopped using credit cards, so Nancy had no way of knowing where he had gone next. The police couldn't help her. Because he had left voluntarily, they had no reason to keep looking for him. He hadn't broken any laws.

As it turned out, Jay had gone to El Paso, Texas. He later tried to explain why he had skipped out. He said, "It's part of life, experimentation. If life isn't interesting and a little bit exciting, you're missing a lot." He also said, "I went into what I did with both feet flying and a great sense of anticipation of what was going to happen next. It's not the knowing. It's the not knowing that's exciting."

While in San Diego, Jay saw an ad for a $69 plane fare to El Paso. He thought that sounded pretty good, so off he went. In El Paso, he took the name Jay Martin Adams. He became a regular at a bar there, quickly forming a new network of friends among the patrons. Phyllis Peterson was one of these new friends. According to her, "He showed up one day and became part of us." She said he was "obviously well-educated, charming, fun to be with. You know, fit right in."

Connie Day was another new buddy. She said Jay was "rather like a grain of rice. You could take him and put him in any situation, and he would just blend right in."

Jay fell in love with Dawn Garcia, one of the women from the bar. Six months after he arrived in El Paso, it looked as if he had succeeded in starting a new life. Then *People* magazine ran a story about Jay Carsey's disappearance. It included a picture of him. When his El Paso friends saw the magazine, Jay's cover was blown. Dawn, however, didn't care. She loved him no matter who he was or what his past had been.

Now that his real identity had been revealed, Jay decided to divorce Nancy and marry Dawn. He also went back to work in college administration. In 1988, he became an adviser to the vice-president of El Paso Community College. His colleagues there loved him. They called him "charismatic" and "brilliant." But on December 22, 1992, Jay did it again. He drove to the airport, parked his car, and hopped on the next plane out of town.

Like Nancy, Dawn was heartbroken. But she wasn't as shocked as Nancy had been. She said she had known all along that Jay was a "free spirit." Still, she was very sad. She said, "I'm only sorry he didn't ask me to run away with him. I would have done it."

This time Jay had only $2,500 with him. He checked into a cheap hotel in Jacksonville, Florida. He sent a note to Dawn telling her she could have everything he had left behind. Then, once again, he began to build a new life. He got a job teaching math at St. Leo College. He fell in love with a woman named Corinne Silverton. For seven years, Jay Carsey stayed in Jacksonville. He might have picked up and left again, but he ran out of time. On August 20, 2000, at the age of sixty-five, Jay Carsey died.

If you have been timed while reading this article, enter your reading time below. Then turn to the Words-per-Minute Table on page 120 and look up your reading speed (words per minute). Enter your reading speed on the graph on page 121.

Reading Time: Selection 2

_____ : _____
MINUTES   SECONDS

UNDERSTANDING IDEAS Circle the letter of the best answer.

1. **Jay Carsey disappeared because he**

   A had been kidnapped

   B had been in a bad accident

   C wanted a more exciting life

   D did not want to upset his wife

2. **Which picture BEST describes what Jay Carsey left behind for his wife, Nancy?**

   1 a note

   2 a lot of money

   3 a car

   4 credit cards

   F Picture 1

   G Picture 2

   H Picture 3

   J Picture 4

3. **Jay Carsey was discovered in El Paso when**

   A he used a credit card with his real name on it

   B the police spotted him

   C Dawn Garcia figured out who he was

   D *People* magazine ran an article about him

4. **Based on the story, which statement do you think is true?**

   F Jay Carsey probably would have left Corrine Silverton.

   G Jay Carsey would never have left Corrine Silverton.

   H Jay Carsey believed in staying with one partner for life.

   J Jay Carsey did not like to experiment with new ideas.

SUMMARIZE For each blank, choose the word that best completes the meaning of the paragraph.

name	flight	story
recognized	returned	blend

Jay Carsey got on a plane in 1982 and never

_____ home. He went to San

Diego and saw an ad for a _____

to El Paso, Texas. There he changed his

_____ and began a new life. The

people he met liked him a lot and later said that he could

_____ into any situation. Then

People magazine ran a _____

about Jay's disappearance. His new friends

_____ him and his cover was

blown.

IF YOU WERE THERE Imagine that someone you were very close to disappeared. Write a brief paragraph explaining your actions. Be sure to include examples from the story to support your response.

_____

_____

_____

_____

_____

_____

USE CONTEXT CLUES When you read, you may find a word whose meaning is unfamiliar to you. When that happens, you can look up the word's meaning in the dictionary. You can also find out what the word means by looking for context clues. These are words or sentences that come before or after the word. Context clues can be synonyms or antonyms of the unfamiliar word. They may also be an example or definition of the unfamiliar word.

Read each excerpt from the stories you just read. Circle the letter with the best meaning of the underlined word.

1. He <u>slipped</u> out of bed in the middle of the night without waking his wife, Jane Noble.

   A slid away quietly

   B fell

   C jumped

   D ran quickly

2. Then the police found his T-shirt. It had <u>washed</u> up on shore near his car. Jane fell apart. To her, this was evidence that Matthew had drowned in the sea.

   F rubbed

   G scrubbed

   H moved by water

   J cleaned

3. They [the police] suspected he had run off and started a new life, leaving Jane—and everyone else he knew—behind. Without <u>proof</u>, of course, they couldn't be sure.

   A doubt

   B guess

   C hope

   D evidence

4. She hoped the pictures might spur Matthew to return. "I just want Matthew to get in <u>touch</u>," she told reporters.

   F contact

   G skill

   H pat

   J trace

5. He had stopped using credit cards, so Nancy had no way of knowing where he had gone next. The police couldn't help her. Because he had left <u>voluntarily</u>, they had no reason to keep looking for him.

   A quickly

   B by his own choice

   C smoothly

   D against his will

PUT WORDS INTO CONTEXT Complete the paragraph using the underlined words from the exercise on this page.

When a loved one disappears, family and friends look

for _____ that the person is still

alive. But what happens when the person has

left _____? What if there is no

kidnapping or murder, rather the person simply

_____ away in the night? Family

members may plead with the person to get in

_____, but the missing person is

seldom heard from again.

SYNONYMS

SYNONYMS A synonym is a word that has the same, or nearly the same, meaning as another word. For example, *happy* and *glad* are synonyms.

Circle the letter of the word that has almost the SAME meaning as the underlined word.

1. **Then he drove to the airport and caught a plane out of town, never to return.**

   A hooked

   B arrived

   C took

   D captured

2. **But that day's mail brought news she never expected: he had left of his own accord.**

   F free choice

   G harmony

   H protest

   J refusal

3. **Wanting to know where he had gone and why, Nancy tried to track his moves.**

   A predict

   B forget

   C follow

   D lose

4. **"You could just take him and put him in any situation, and he would just blend right in."**

   F separate

   G fit

   H split

   J divide

5. **He checked into a cheap hotel in Jacksonville.**

   A large

   B fancy

   C clean

   D inexpensive

SYNONYM ANALOGIES

SYNONYM ANALOGIES Analogies show relationships between words. Synonym analogies show patterns between words that have similar meanings. For example, *big* is to *large* as *little* is to *small*. For each blank, choose a word from the exercise on this page that correctly completes the analogy.

1. *Costly* is to *expensive* as *low price* is to

   _____ .

2. *Toss* is to *throw* as *hunt* is to

   _____ .

3. *Snared* is to *captured* as *grabbed* is to

   _____ .

4. *Separate* is to *divide* as *mix* is to

   _____ .

ORGANIZE IDEAS The main ideas in a story are the larger, more general topics that are covered. The specific details are the facts that clarify or support the main idea. Fill in the chart by using the items listed at the right. If the bulleted item is a main idea from the story, write it in the row marked "Main Idea." If the item is a detail that supports the main idea, write it in the row marked "Detail."

"A Doctor Ducks Out"
Main Idea:
Detail:
Detail:
Detail:
Detail:

"Like a Grain of Rice"
Main Idea:
Detail:
Detail:
Detail:
Detail:

- Jay Carsey withdrew $30,000 in cash from a secret bank account.

- Police found Matthew's T-shirt on the shore near his car.

- On August 20, 2000, Jay Carsey died.

- Jay married Dawn Garcia, but four years later he left her.

- The police did not think Matthew committed suicide.

- Matthew and Jane were both doctors.

- Dawn was not surprised that Jay left.

- Jane moved to Australia with their son.

- Matthew Choyce disappeared and tried to make it look like he committed suicide.

- Jay Carsey's idea of excitement was to leave his life behind and start over.

SUPPORT THE MAIN IDEA Write a paragraph about someone who has disappeared. State the main idea in the first sentence. Then use details from both stories to support your main idea.

_____

_____

_____

_____

_____

_____

_____

DRAW CONCLUSIONS A conclusion is a judgment based on information. The way you draw a conclusion is to think about what you've read and to see if you can make a judgment, or general statement, about it. Read this paragraph about people who have left their families behind. Then choose the best answer for each question.

[1] Sometimes people just decide to leave their spouses and disappear. [2] Men between 26 and 35 are most likely to do this and twice as likely as women. [3] Some people try to make their disappearance look like a suicide. [4] In some cases, the missing person is discovered in a new place. [5] Some people repeat the pattern by beginning a new life over and over.

1. **Which conclusion can you draw based on the paragraph above?**

   A Women are less likely than men to disappear.

   B Men are less likely than women to disappear.

   C Most of the people who have disappeared have committed suicide.

   D Older men are most likely to leave their families behind.

2. **Which sentence from the paragraph identifies who is most likely to leave their family?**

   F Sentence 1

   G Sentence 2

   H Sentence 3

   J Sentence 4

3. **Which sentence helps you conclude if someone will disappear more than once?**

   A Sentence 2

   B Sentence 3

   C Sentence 4

   D Sentence 5

JUDGE THE EVIDENCE When you make a conclusion, you must judge if the information presented is accurate or convincing. Choose the best answer.

1. **Which statement best supports the conclusion that Matthew Choyce planned to leave his wife?**

   A He and Jane were about to have a baby.

   B He never came back.

   C He was looking for a new job.

   D He left a note on the front seat of his car.

2. **Which statement best supports the conclusion that Jay Carsey's first wife Nancy was upset when he left?**

   F She added, "It was like a nightmare that wouldn't stop."

   G He told Nancy he would be home for lunch.

   H She could tell that Jay had written the note.

   J Nancy tried to track his moves.

YOUR OWN CONCLUSION Pretend that you are part of the Newcastle police force and must decide whether Matthew Choyce committed suicide or not. State your conclusion and support it with examples from the story.

_____

_____

_____

_____

_____

_____

_____

SELECTION 1

Shark Attack

Ten-year-old Brendan Flosenzier was the first one to see the shark. Brendan and his family were at the beach near Pensacola, Florida, on July 6, 2001. Brendan wasn't in deep water. He was only fifteen yards from shore, floating on a raft in two and a half feet of water. His cousins, Vincent and Jessie Arbogast, were playing in the water near him. Suddenly Brendan saw a seven-foot bull shark swim by. It brushed against nine-year-old Vincent and kept going. Before either boy had time to react, the shark opened its jaws and attacked Vincent's eight-year-old brother, Jessie.

"Shark!" Brendan screamed.

Back on shore, Jessie's uncle, Vance Flosenzier, heard the cry. He jumped up and raced into the water.

Jessie saw Vance coming. "He's got me!" the boy shouted. "Get him off me!"

That's just what Vance wanted to do. As he splashed toward Jessie, he saw the water turning red with blood. The shark had bitten a huge chunk out of Jessie's leg. Now it had Jessie's arm clenched in its razor-sharp teeth. Vance didn't stop to think. He did the only thing he could think of to try to save Jessie. He grabbed the shark by the tail and started pulling. As he did so, the shark bit Jessie's arm off just below the shoulder. But Vance held on. He managed to move the 200-pound shark away from his nephew. Amazingly, he pulled the shark all the way to shore.

Vance's heroic actions gave Jessie a chance for survival—but only a small one. Blood was pouring out of the gash in Jessie's leg. He was turning white as all the blood drained from his body.

Just then a man came rushing out into the water. He had been walking on the beach and had heard the boys' screams. Without thinking of his own safety, he ran out to help. The man picked Jessie up and carried him to shore. He placed Jessie in the arms of Vance's wife, Diana. Then this man, whom Diana called "Jessie's guardian angel," ran off to call 911.

Luckily, Diana knew how to do CPR. So did a beachgoer named Susanne Werton, who stepped up to help her. Werton later described just how bad Jessie looked. "It was truly unbelievable," she said. "He was lying there with no arm, the whole right side of his leg was gone and there wasn't even any blood. . . . His lips were pure white; his eyes were wide open but rolled back into his head."

The two women pushed on Jessie's chest and blew air into his lungs. Then a LifeFlight helicopter arrived. The paramedics took one look at Jessie and knew they had to get him to the hospital right away. Diana said, "It was Friday night in the summer on Pensacola Beach, and it would have taken an ambulance a half-hour to get there. The helicopter was there in two minutes. He wouldn't have had a chance if he'd had to go by ambulance."

As Jessie was airlifted to Baptist Hospital, others turned their attention to the shark. Vance had pulled it up onto the sand, but it was still alive—and Jessie's arm was inside it. Park ranger Jared Klein wanted to get the arm. He thought perhaps doctors could reattach it. Klein tried to pry the shark's mouth open, but it snapped its teeth shut. Klein pulled out his gun and shot it four times in the head. Then he held its mouth open with his baton while a lifeguard named Tony Thomas reached down the shark's throat and managed to grab Jessie's arm.

Jessie arrived at the hospital long before his arm did. But doctors had other things to worry about besides the missing limb. Jessie had lost almost all the blood in his body. For thirty minutes, his brain had been without oxygen. Doctors quickly pumped new blood into him. They managed to get his system going again. But he was in a coma. They weren't sure if he would ever come out of it.

Ambulance workers brought in Jessie's arm. Doctors spent eleven hours trying to reattach it. It wasn't easy. They had to reconnect nerves, muscles, and tissue. At last they finished. They could not tell if Jessie would ever get back the use of his fingers, but they had saved his arm and hand.

Fortunately, the rest of his recovery was not so dramatic. In time, Jessie did stir from his coma. But progress was very slow. For months, his parents weren't sure if he recognized them. It was six months before he said a single word. A year after the accident, he still wasn't able to talk much. He had regained some use of his arms and legs, but he wasn't strong enough to walk. It wasn't clear whether his brain would ever bounce back.

Still, Jessie's family chose to focus on the positive. By the summer of 2002, Jessie had grown an inch and a half. "That's one of the things that give us hope that his brain will recover," said Diana.

Even if he never made a full recovery, the people who loved Jessie were grateful that he was alive. One woman who knew Jessie said, "When you think of all that he's been through, he's really our own little miracle."

If you have been timed while reading this article, enter your reading time below. Then turn to the Words-per-Minute Table on page 120 and look up your reading speed (words per minute). Enter your reading speed on the graph on page 121.

Reading Time: Selection 1

_____ : _____
MINUTES   SECONDS

UNDERSTANDING IDEAS Circle the letter of the best answer.

1. Which statement belongs in the empty box?

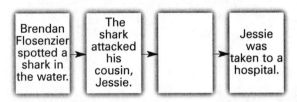

Brendan Flosenzier spotted a shark in the water. → The shark attacked his cousin, Jessie. → [ ] → Jessie was taken to a hospital.

A A seven-foot bull shark swam past Brendan.

B Jessie did not speak for six months after the attack.

C Vance pulled the shark to shore.

D Jessie had grown an inch and a half.

2. What did Diana Flosenzier and Susanne Werton do to help Jessie?

F They performed CPR.

G They called 911.

H They pulled Jessie's arm out of the shark.

J They put him in the helicopter.

3. Diana called a man on the beach "Jessie's guardian angel" because he

A performed CPR on Jessie

B killed the shark

C pulled Jessie out of the water and called 911

D was a doctor who could treat Jessie

4. Which statement about Jessie's experience is correct?

F Jessie was never able to speak again.

G He survived the attack but hasn't made a full recovery.

H He almost died because nobody helped him.

J Jessie was able to fight off the shark.

SUMMARIZE For each blank, choose the word that best completes the meaning of the paragraph.

shark	attacked	save
beach	helicopter	swimming

On July 6, 2001, Brendan Flosenzier was

_____ at a beach in Florida.

Suddenly he screamed, "_____!"

A seven-foot bull shark _____ his

cousin, Jessie. Vance Flosenzier raced into the water to

try to _____ Jessie from the shark.

He was able to pull the shark up onto the

_____. Meanwhile, another

man ran to call 911, and soon after a LifeFlight

_____ arrived and took Jessie to

the hospital.

IF YOU WERE THERE Write a brief paragraph explaining what you would do if someone near you was attacked by a shark. Be sure to include examples from the story to support your response.

_____

_____

_____

_____

_____

A Hole in His Head

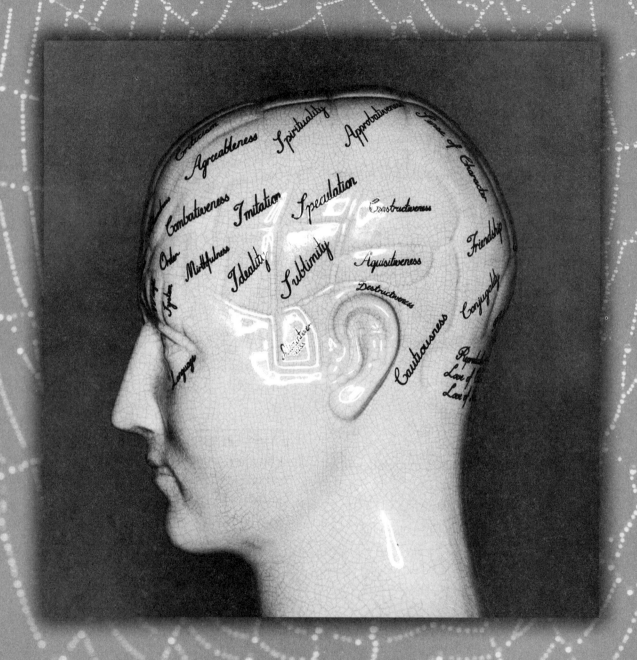

Phineas Gage was good at his job. At the age of twenty-five, he had already risen to the rank of foreman for the Rutland and Burlington Railroad. His bosses viewed him as one of their very best workers. But on September 13, 1848, Gage made a mistake. It was a terrible, hideous mistake. And although it didn't kill him, it changed him forever. Afterwards, his friends all agreed that "Gage was no longer Gage."

The day began as usual. Gage was working in Cavendish, Vermont. He and his crew were getting ready to dynamite through some rocks. Gage was carrying a long metal rod called a tamping iron. It was about the size of a broom handle, but one end was filed down to a sharp point. It was quite heavy, weighing more than thirteen pounds. Gage used the blunt end of this tool to push dynamite gently down into holes in the ground.

On this day, though, Gage was not careful enough with his tamping iron. Somehow it slipped out of his hand. It dropped down into a hole where some dynamite had been placed. The rod hit the dynamite hard, causing it to explode. That sent the tamping iron flying out of the hole like a missile. It flew right toward Gage's head. The pointed end pierced his cheek right below his left eye. The entire rod shot through his skull, came out at the top of his head, and sailed another ninety feet before landing on the ground.

The force of the blow knocked Gage over. As the rod passed through his head, it destroyed his left eye. It also blew out much of the front part of his brain. But, amazingly, it didn't kill him. In fact, as his horrified co-workers loaded him onto an oxcart, Gage sat up and began talking. Blood was pouring from the hole in his head and he was clearly in a state of shock. Still, when he got to town he was able to climb out of the oxcart on his own. He walked up a whole flight of stairs to the doctor's office. He then proceeded to tell Dr. John Martyn Harlow what had happened to him.

Harlow could hardly believe it. Such an accident should have killed Gage instantly. As Harlow examined him, he could see Gage's brain clearly through the opening in the skull. The doctor did his best to close and bandage the wound. Then he sat back and hoped for the best.

Over the next couple of days, Gage's condition worsened. He was weak from the loss of blood. Also, his wounds became infected. But slowly he did recover. Ten weeks after the accident, he was well enough to travel to Lebanon, New Hampshire. There he continued to rest and heal at his mother's house.

Friends and relatives considered his survival to be something of a miracle. So did his doctor. Gage's left cheek would always look sunken, and his left eye was gone. He also had a large dent on the top of his head where a piece of his skull was missing. Still, he looked fairly normal. Even more surprising, perhaps, was the fact that his intellectual abilities were unimpaired. He could add and subtract just as well as ever. He had no problem remembering names and dates. He could carry out complex orders and recall detailed information.

So, on the surface, Phineas Gage had defied death. He had suffered a deadly injury, yet emerged essentially intact. Or had he? As time passed, it became clear to Gage's friends that something was wrong.

For one thing, Gage now swore. In the past, he had been a courteous young man. Now he was quite foul-mouthed. He was rude to people for no reason, often shouting at them and calling them names. Before the accident he had been calm and patient. He had been described as even-tempered. Now little things irritated him. He flew into a rage easily and seemed to change his mind constantly. Gage's contemporaries didn't know much about how the brain worked. But they rightly guessed that Gage's injury was the cause of the changes. He had lost the part of his brain that controlled social behavior.

Several months after the accident, Gage felt strong enough to return to work. But his bosses hesitated. They could tell he wasn't the same person as before. And the more they saw of this new Gage, the less they liked him. In the end, they decided they just couldn't give him his job back.

No one else wanted to hire Gage, either. He was no fun to be around. Certainly he could no longer be put in charge of other people. At last he got a job caring for horses in a stable. Over the next ten years, he drifted from New Hampshire to South America and then to California. In each of these places he found jobs working with horses. In early 1860, Gage began to have epileptic seizures. His overall level of health declined. On May 21, at the age of thirty-seven, Gage died. He had lived twelve years after his horrible accident. But in some ways, the real Phineas Gage died on September 13, 1848.

If you have been timed while reading this article, enter your reading time below. Then turn to the Words-per-Minute Table on page 120 and look up your reading speed (words per minute). Enter your reading speed on the graph on page 121.

Reading Time: Selection 2

_____ : _____
MINUTES   SECONDS

UNDERSTANDING IDEAS Circle the letter of the best answer.

1. **What happened to Phineas Gage on September 13, 1848?**

   A He had a terrible accident.

   B He fell off a ladder and hit his head.

   C He began using foul language.

   D He was killed in an accident.

2. **Phineas Gage's doctor**

   F thought Gage had a minor injury

   G had seen several other patients with the same type of injury

   H was amazed Gage was alive

   J could not see Gage's brain through the hole in his head

3. **Gage's friends knew something was wrong because he**

   A was courteous and calm

   B was rude and impatient

   C had stopped swearing

   D could no longer add or subtract

4. **Gage worked with horses because**

   F he began to have epileptic seizures

   G he was such a good rider

   H people did not like being around him

   J he didn't want his old job

SUMMARIZE For each blank, choose the word that best completes the meaning of the paragraph.

dynamite	eye	
		normal
mistake	swear	

On September 13, 1848, Phineas Gage made a

terrible _____. He accidentally

exploded some _____, which sent a

metal rod through his head. The rod destroyed his left

_____ but did not kill him. In fact,

he first seemed _____.

However, his friends noticed that he had begun to

_____ and had become very

irritable.

IF YOU WERE THERE If you were Gage's old employer, would you let him have his job back? Write a brief paragraph explaining what you would do and why. Be sure to include examples from the story to support your response.

_____

_____

_____

_____

_____

USE CONTEXT CLUES When you read, you may find a word whose meaning is unfamiliar to you. When that happens, you can look up the word's meaning in the dictionary. You can also find out what the word means by looking for context clues. These are words or sentences that come before or after the word. Context clues can be synonyms or antonyms of the unfamiliar word. They may also be an example or definition of the unfamiliar word.

Read each excerpt from the stories you just read. Circle the letter with the best meaning of the underlined word.

1. **The shark had bitten a huge chunk out of Jessie's leg. Now it had Jessie's arm clenched in its razor-sharp teeth.**

   A held tightly

   B broken

   C hurt badly

   D cleaned

2. **Jessie arrived at the hospital long before his arm did. But doctors had other things to worry about besides the missing limb.**

   F twig

   G branch of a tree

   H human arm or leg

   J bough

3. **He had regained some use of his arms and legs. . . . By the summer of 2002, Jessie had grown an inch and a half. "That's one of the things that give us hope that his brain will recover," said Diana.**

   A grow

   B heal

   C worsen

   D live

4. **The rod hit the dynamite hard, causing it to explode. That sent the tamping iron flying out of the hole like a missile.**

   F power to fly

   G explosive

   H something terrific

   J wonderful

5. **The entire rod shot through his skull, came out at the top of his head, and sailed another 90 feet before landing on the ground. The force of the blow knocked George over.**

   A hit

   B gale

   C puff

   D fortune

PUT WORDS INTO CONTEXT Complete the paragraph using the underlined words from the exercise on this page.

An accident can happen at any time.

While walking in a forest, you might get your leg

_____ in an animal trap.

While watching a baseball game, you might get a

_____ to the head from a stray ball.

Or, you might lose a _____ in a car

accident. Whatever happens, you have the best chance

to _____ from your injuries if the

paramedics treat you immediately.

PREFIXES A prefix is one or more letters added to the beginning of a word to change its meaning. For example, the prefix *non-* means "not." The word *toxic* means "poisonous." So, when you add the prefix *non-* to the beginning of the word *toxic*, you get *nontoxic*, which means "not poisonous."

Use a dictionary to find the meaning of each prefix below. Match the prefix with its meaning on the right. Examples for each definition are included in italics. Write the letter of the correct definition on the line. **One of the definitions will be used twice.**

_____ **1.** para-

_____ **2.** un-

_____ **3.** re-

_____ **4.** dis-

_____ **5.** de-

_____ **6.** co-

_____ **7.** fore-

A not: *uncommon*

B front, first: *foresight*

C again: *resale*

D related or similar to: *paraphrase*

E with, together: *cohabit*

F do the opposite of: *disconnect, decertify*

WRITE DEFINITIONS In the exercise below, underline the prefix and write the new meaning of the word on the line provided.

1. un + believeable = unbelievable

definition: _____

2. para + medics = paramedics

definition: _____

3. de + criminalize = decriminalize

definition: _____

4. re + attach = reattach

definition: _____

5. fore + man = foreman

definition: _____

6. co + worker = coworker

definition: _____

7. dis + believe = disbelieve

definition: _____

ORGANIZE THE FACTS A summary of a story is a retelling of the major points of the story. Minor details and examples are not included. To write a summary, first you must decide what the most important points are. You can do this by making a list. Then write a paragraph using the main points from your list. The paragraph is your summary.

Look at the major points listed under "Shark Attack." Fill in the missing information. Then list the major points of "A Hole in His Head."

"Shark Attack"
1. On July 6, 2001, a shark attacked 8-year-old Jessie Arbogast in Pensacola, Florida.
2. Vance grabbed the shark and pulled it to shore.
3. A man carried Jessie out of the water and called 911.
4. A rescue helicopter flew Jessie to a hospital where they reattached his arm.
5.

"A Hole in His Head"
1. In 1848, Phineas Gage had a terrible accident.
2.
3.
4.
5.

COMPARE THE STORIES Using the major points listed above, write a brief paragraph summarizing "A Hole in His Head."

_____

_____

_____

_____

_____

_____

_____

MAKE PREDICTIONS You can make predictions, or educated guesses, based on what you already know. For example, you know that there is a traffic jam on the main highway every day at rush hour between five and six o'clock in the evening. Based on this knowledge, you can reasonably predict that tomorrow's rush hour traffic will be the same way. Read this passage, and answer the following questions based on what you know.

Fast Ball

Jimmy Rivera threw the next pitch. It was his best fastball. The batter swung hard and hit the ball like a rocket right back at Jimmy. The ball hit him in the forehead, and Jimmy fell to the ground and did not move. People gathered around right away to see how he was. He was unconscious and didn't seem to be breathing.

---

1. **Based on the stories you have read in this unit, what do you predict is the first thing that someone would do to help Jimmy?**

   A drive him to the hospital

   B give him CPR

   C take him to a nearby doctor

   D take him home

2. **What do you predict someone might do to help Jimmy next?**

   F make him sit up

   G carry him off the field

   H call 911

   J try to get him to eat something

JUDGE THE BASIS OF A PREDICTION For predictions to be reasonably accurate, they must be based on what you know as factual information. Use the stories you just read to help you predict what will happen to Jimmy. Choose the best answer.

1. **Which of the below helps you predict the first thing done to help Jimmy?**

   A Jessie was immediately given CPR.

   B Jessie's cousin was near him when the shark attacked.

   C Phineas Gage was able to talk after his accident.

   D Jessie's and Phineas' lives were both changed after their accidents.

2. **Which statement helps you predict what might happen to Jimmy if his personality changed for the worse after his accident?**

   F Gage worked on a railroad.

   G Gage traveled from place to place.

   H Gage was putting dynamite into the ground.

   J None of his friends liked the new Gage, and he lost his job.

PREDICT WHAT YOU WOULD DO Write a brief paragraph explaining what you would do if a good friend had a very bad accident. Use examples from the stories you just read to explain your decisions.

_____

_____

_____

_____

_____

_____

SELECTION 1

No One Noticed

Peter Vella wanted the lawn of his Chicago home to look nice. He always kept it neatly mowed. His elderly neighbor, Adolph Stec, on the other hand, didn't seem to care what his yard looked like. In the summer of 1997, Stec didn't mow his lawn once.

"The grass in his yard got as high as two feet," said Vella. "So I mowed his, too. I didn't want the neighborhood to go to pot."

For four years, Vella mowed his neighbor's yard. Stec never once said "thank you." But it turned out that Stec had a good excuse. For the entire four years, he was sitting in his living room, dead.

Stec had never been a friendly fellow, and after his long-time girlfriend died in 1996, he became more withdrawn than ever. When he expired in his chair, no one missed him. "He must have abandoned the place, we thought," said neighbor Cathy Rosario.

Because Stec was no longer paying his taxes, the government took ownership of the house. It sold the building for back taxes. A man named Ronald Ohr bought it without ever going inside. In May 2001, Ohr walked into it for the first time. He saw Stec's body in a chair in the living room. Nearby was a newspaper and a calendar dating back to February 1997.

"All we can do is feel sorry for the man," said Ohr's wife, Jeanne. "It makes you appreciate the fact that you have loved ones."

Adolph Stec was not the only person who ever died unnoticed. In Germany, a man lay dead in his home for four years without anyone knowing. When he stopped paying his bills, the electric company cut off the power. Everyone thought the place was empty. A real estate agent discovered the grisly truth after someone expressed an interest in buying the building.

The same thing happened to Wolfgang Dircks. He died in 1993, but no one found out until 1998. Dircks was only 43 at the time of his death. He had stopped working because of a bad hip. After his wife left him, Dircks became bitter and reclusive. He told everyone to leave him alone. So they did. His elderly mother stopped calling him. Neighbors stopped checking on him. In addition, Dircks arranged his life so that he never had to leave his apartment. He had his monthly bills paid directly from his bank account. When he needed groceries, he had them delivered from a nearby market.

On December 5, 1993, Dircks died. He was sitting in a chair watching TV at the time. He had the list of that day's TV programs on his lap. He also had his Christmas tree lights on. At some point after his death, the TV blew a fuse. But for the next five years, the Christmas lights stayed on. These lights could be seen from the street, but most people paid no attention. One man did notice them twinkling. He mentioned it to the building manager. The manager didn't know why Dircks would leave his holiday lights on. But the manager figured it was none of his business.

Dircks' death might have gone unnoticed forever except that his bank account finally ran out. That meant the landlord stopped getting the monthly rent. The landlord wanted to know what was going on, so he went to see Dircks. That's when he found his skeleton in the chair.

Incidents like this make splashy headlines. Critics point to them as evidence that there isn't enough human contact in daily life anymore. They say people now live "next to each other" instead of "with each other."

"More and more people are leading isolated lives," says Ralph Kirscht, director of a counseling center in Bonn, Germany.

That may be true. But most people would still be shocked to come across a dead body in someone's home. Such a discovery certainly shocked two men in Prince Rupert, British Columbia. They were thieves. On December 31, 2001, they broke into the home of an elderly man named Filippo Falcone. They found Falcone's body lying on the floor of his bedroom. He had been dead for a long time.

The two thieves panicked. They didn't know what to do. At last one of them picked up the phone and called the police.

"They were quite horrified to discover the deceased in the bedroom," said police officer Lance Stewart. He added that the two thieves "quickly forgot about their purpose in being in the house."

The story of Filippo Falcone surprised people in Prince Rupert. But Ralph Kirscht wasn't surprised. Said Kirscht, "It's perverse that people can die and no one notices. But it happens all the time."

If you have been timed while reading this article, enter your reading time below. Then turn to the Words-per-Minute Table on page 120 and look up your reading speed (words per minute). Enter your reading speed on the graph on page 121.

Reading Time: Selection 1

_____ : _____
MINUTES   SECONDS

UNDERSTANDING IDEAS Circle the letter of the best answer.

1. **Adolph Stec never mowed his lawn because he**

   A was traveling overseas

   B had moved

   C had died

   D didn't care about his yard

2. **Wolfgang Dircks was discovered five years after he died because**

   F his bank account ran out of money

   G neighbors came in to investigate

   H thieves found him in his apartment

   J his television set was on

3. **After breaking into Filippo Falcone's home, thieves found**

   A diamonds and gold

   B a lighted Christmas tree

   C stacks of dollar bills

   D a dead body

4. **Which of the following best summarizes the story you just read?**

   F It is sad when someone dies and nobody notices, but it happens often.

   G People never die without someone noticing.

   H People die in many different ways.

   J Fewer people die alone in Germany than in the United States.

SUMMARIZE For each blank, choose the word that best completes the meaning of the paragraph.

abandoned	dead	bought
calendar	taxes	body

Peter Vella never noticed that his neighbor was sitting in his living room _____

for four years. Other neighbors thought that Stec

had _____ his house.

Finally, the government sold the building for

back _____. A man

_____ the house without seeing

the inside. When the buyer finally went into the house,

he found Stec's _____. Near the

body was a _____ and newspaper

dating back four years.

IF YOU WERE THERE Write a brief paragraph explaining what you would do if you stopped seeing one of your neighbors. Be sure to include examples from the story to support your response.

_____

_____

_____

_____

Strange Tales of Death

All deaths are sad. But let's face it: some are also weird. Throughout history, people have died in all sorts of bizarre ways. Consider the famous Greek poet Aeschylus. He died around 500 B.C. According to legend, Aeschylus was outside one day when an eagle mistook his head for a rock. The eagle was carrying a tortoise in its claws. It was looking for some place to drop the tortoise so the shell would break open and it could feed on the meat. When the eagle spotted the top of Aeschylus's head, it believed it had found the perfect rock. It opened its claws and dropped the tortoise right onto the head of the unsuspecting poet. Aeschylus is said to have died instantly.

It wasn't a nearsighted eagle that killed Sir Francis Bacon; it was a chicken. To be more specific, it was a frozen chicken. In March of 1626, the English scientist was working on the concept of frozen food. He wanted to see how long chicken meat would last if it was packed in snow. He was filling the chicken carcass with snow when a blizzard hit. Bacon was out in the elements long enough to catch pneumonia. He was sick for a month. But in the end, pneumonia killed him.

A toothpick turned out to be a deadly weapon for American writer Sherwood Anderson. In 1941, Anderson was heading out on a trip to South America. He went to a farewell party just before he left. The food looked good, so Anderson helped himself. At one point, he used a toothpick to pick up one of the snacks. As he nibbled it, he bit off a piece of the toothpick. This small piece of wood lodged in his intestines. The area became inflamed. As infection set in, Anderson grew sicker and sicker. He died on board the ship that was taking him to Brazil.

The always-dangerous light bulb killed French musician Claude François. He had just taken a shower and had noticed that the light over his head wasn't working. He got a new bulb and climbed back into the bathtub to change it. The bottom of the tub was still wet, however. When François touched the light socket, he was electrocuted.

Writer Tennessee Williams was already in bed when he died. He wasn't doing anything dangerous—or so he thought. Apparently Williams had a stuffy nose. He picked up a bottle of nose spray. But the cap of the bottle fell off and dropped into his mouth. He choked to death on the cap.

Actor Jon-Erik Hexum was working on a TV show when he died. The show called for some shooting scenes, so there were some prop guns on the set. One day Hexum was joking around. He picked up one of the guns and put it to his head. Knowing that it held blanks, he went ahead and pulled the trigger. What Hexum didn't know was that even a blank can be deadly. Although there was no bullet in the gun, the gunpowder exploded with such force that it fractured Hexum's skull. He lasted six days in a coma before doctors pronounced him dead.

Another actor, Anthony Dwain Lee, lost his life in a different kind of shooting accident. On Halloween of 2000, Lee was at a party in Los Angeles. Most people there were in costume. Lee was dressed in a black sweatshirt and black vest, and was carrying a toy gun. Around 1:00 A.M., neighbors complained that the party was getting too loud. Police came to check things out. That's when Lee made his fatal mistake. Perhaps he thought the officers were just guests in costume. In any case, he pulled out his toy gun and pointed it at Officer Tarriel Hopper. Thinking that Lee was going to shoot him, Hopper drew his weapon. He shot and killed Lee on the spot.

Pointing a toy gun at an officer may be stupid, but so is standing up on a ride at Disneyland. In 1964, 15-year-old

Mark Maples was riding Disney's Matterhorn Bobsled ride. As his car neared the top of the mountain, Maples took off his seat belt and stood up. He lost his balance and was thrown out of the car onto the track below. He died three days later from his injuries.

The list goes on and on. Dancer Isadora Duncan was killed by a long scarf she was wearing. One end of it got caught in the wheels of her sports car, strangling her. Guitarist Merle Watson died when his tractor rolled over him. And bungee jumper Hal Mark Irish died when he slipped out of his bungee cord.

In some ways, jockey Frank Hayes' death was the most unusual. Hayes had a heart attack in the middle of a horse race. He died in the saddle before the race ended. But his horse, named Sweet Kiss, just kept running. Sweet Kiss crossed the finish line and won the race. That made Hayes the only dead jockey ever to win a horse race. It also showed that no matter what form death takes, life does go on.

If you have been timed while reading this article, enter your reading time below. Then turn to the Words-per-Minute Table on page 120 and look up your reading speed (words per minute). Enter your reading speed on the graph on page 121.

Reading Time: Selection 2

_____ : _____
MINUTES   SECONDS

UNDERSTANDING IDEAS Circle the letter of the best answer.

1. **According to the article, which statement is true?**

   A If a gun has blanks in it, it is perfectly safe.

   B You should never use a toothpick.

   C Some people die in very strange ways.

   D It's worse to be killed by an eagle than to die in bed.

2. **Claude François was killed because he**

   F thought frozen meat might last longer than unfrozen meat

   G was trying to catch an eagle in the wild

   H pointed a toy gun at a policeman

   J tried to change a light bulb while standing in a wet bathtub

3. **The writer Tennessee Williams was lying in bed when he**

   A accidentally shot himself with a gun

   B choked to death by swallowing a bottle cap

   C was strangled to death by his scarf

   D was struck in the head by a tortoise

4. **The article suggests that jockey Frank Hayes' death was the most unusual because**

   F he died but his body was riding the winning horse

   G he died unexpectedly

   H he was a jockey

   J no matter what form death takes, it is the end of life

SUMMARIZE For each blank, choose the word that best completes the meaning of the paragraph.

strangled	blanks	
eagle	died	toothpick

Throughout history, people have

_____ in many strange ways.

The Greek poet Aeschylus died when an

_____ dropped a tortoise on his

head. Sherwood Anderson died after swallowing a piece

of a _____, which infected his

intestines. A television actor jokingly shot himself with a

pistol loaded with _____ and died

six days later. The dancer Isadora Duncan was

_____ to death when her scarf

caught in the wheel of her moving car.

IF YOU WERE THERE Imagine that you are with one of the people whose death is described in the article just before he or she died. Write a brief paragraph explaining the steps you would take to help. Be sure to include examples from the story to support your response.

_____

_____

_____

_____

_____

USE CONTEXT CLUES When you read, you may find a word whose meaning is unfamiliar to you. When that happens, you can look up the word's meaning in the dictionary. You can also find out what the word means by looking for context clues. These are words or sentences that come before or after the word. Context clues can be synonyms or antonyms of the unfamiliar word. They may also be an example or definition of the unfamiliar word.

Read each excerpt from the stories you just read. Circle the letter with the best meaning of the underlined word.

1. **For the entire four years, [Stec] was still sitting in his living room, dead. . . . When he underline{expired} in his chair, no one missed him.**

   A fell asleep

   B died

   C retired

   D woke up

2. **After his wife left him, he became bitter and reclusive. He told everyone to leave him alone.**

   F cruel

   G unhappy

   H wanting to be alone

   J complaining a lot

3. **All deaths are sad, but let's face it: some are also weird. Throughout history, people have died in all sorts of bizarre ways.**

   A common place

   B very unusual

   C terrible

   D wonderful

4. **Bacon was out in the elements long enough to catch pneumonia. He lingered for awhile, but in the end pneumonia killed him.**

   F stayed on, remained

   G slept

   H experimented

   J protested

5. **Although there was no bullet in the gun, the gunpowder exploded with such force that it fractured Hexum's skull.**

   A power

   B noise

   C weakness

   D weight

PUT WORDS INTO CONTEXT Complete the paragraph using the underlined words from the exercise on this page.

Some people die in very _____

ways. For example, one person

_____ in bed choking on the lid of a

bottle. Some people become _____

and no one knows about it when they die. Others have

had accidents but _____ for months

before passing on.

MULTIPLE MEANINGS Some words have several different meanings. You can determine the meaning of a word by seeing how it is used in a sentence.

Read the definitions of each word. On the line, write the meaning of the underlined word as it is used in the sentence.

> **feet:**   **1.** the appendages at the bottom of a leg, used for walking **2.** unit of length that equals twelve inches

1. **The distance between the house and the barn is about 260 <u>feet</u>.**

   _____

2. **When Greg tripped over the invisible wire, his <u>feet</u> quickly went out from under him.**

   _____

> **place:**   **1.** to put something in a spot **2.** a location, city, town, or village

3. **Do you know the name of this <u>place</u>?**

   _____

4. **Miranda asked her brother to <u>place</u> the flowers on the table.**

   _____

> **interest:**   **1.** wanting to know; to be curious **2.** money paid for the use of money

5. **Philip always had a great <u>interest</u> in music.**

   _____

6. **Susanna borrowed the money she needed to start her business because the <u>interest</u> rate was low.**

   _____

> **legend**   **1.** an old story from the past that may or may not be true **2.** words that explain the symbols on a map

7. **There are many <u>legends</u> in the Northwest about a monster called Bigfoot.**

   _____

8. **Jenny was able to find out the size of the city by looking at the <u>legend</u>.**

   _____

> **board**   **1.** meals provided for money **2.** to come alongside or enter a ship

9. **The pirates tried to <u>board</u> the merchant ship but were stopped by the crew.**

   _____

10. **When Laura went to college, she had to pay for her room and <u>board</u>.**

    _____

ORGANIZE THE FACTS The two articles you read in this unit are alike in some ways and different in other ways. A Venn diagram can show how they are alike and different. Look at the Venn diagram below. Then choose the best answer to each question.

"NO ONE NOTICED" — Tells how people died and were not found for a long time

BOTH — About people dying

"STRANGE TALES OF DEATH" — Describes unusual ways that people have died

1. **Which of the following details belongs in the oval marked "BOTH"?**

   A Peter Vella wanted his lawn to look nice.

   B Adolph Stec was found four years after he died.

   C Isadora Duncan was strangled by her own scarf.

   D People can die in strange ways.

2. **Which detail does NOT belong in the oval marked "No One Noticed"?**

   F When someone dies alone it makes us appreciate our loved ones.

   G There isn't enough human contact in daily life anymore.

   H Dircks' bank account ran out of money.

   J Tennessee Williams died in bed by choking.

3. **Which detail does NOT belong in the oval marked "Strange Tales of Death"?**

   A Wolfgang Dircks died while watching TV.

   B Frank Hayes is the only dead jockey to have won a race.

   C Sir Francis Bacon died after getting pneumonia.

   D Hal Mark Irish died while bungee jumping.

COMPARE AND CONTRAST Compare and contrast the two stories by writing a paragraph that supports each of the topic sentences below.

In some ways, the two stories are alike.

_____

_____

_____

_____

_____

In some ways, the two stories are different.

_____

_____

_____

_____

_____

_____

_____

FACT AND OPINION A fact is something you can prove to be true. An opinion is a belief or conclusion that is debatable and cannot be proven to be true.

Read this passage about people dying in strange ways. Then choose the best answer to each question.

[1] People sometimes die in unexpected and unusual ways. [2] It is sad when a person chokes on the lid of a bottle or is strangled by her own scarf. [3] Why can't people be more careful to avoid dangerous situations? [4] Why do people die in what seem to be stupid ways?

1. **Which sentence from the passage states a fact about ways that people die?**

   A Sentence 1

   B Sentence 2

   C Sentence 3

   D Sentence 4

2. **Which sentence from the passage states an opinion about people being more cautious?**

   F Sentence 1

   G Sentence 2

   H Sentence 3

   J Sentence 4

3. **Which of the following statements is an opinion?**

   A People have died in bed or in a bathtub.

   B People have died after being outside in the cold.

   C The most stupid way to die would be getting hit on the head with a tortoise.

   D A woman was strangled with her own scarf.

JUDGE THE EVIDENCE To convince a reader to agree with an opinion, the writer often provides evidence. The reader has to judge if the evidence is adequate to support the opinion. Choose the best answer.

1. **Which statement supports the opinion that changing a light bulb can be dangerous?**

   A If you stand in water and touch a light socket, you can be electrocuted.

   B There are many different styles and colors of light bulbs.

   C Changing a light bulb is a simple thing to do.

   D You should always use a ladder when you change a light bulb.

2. **Which statement supports the opinion that you can die in what seems like a safe place?**

   F Tennessee Williams died in bed.

   G Isadora Duncan died in her sports car.

   H Mark Maples died when he fell out of a roller coaster.

   J Hal Mark Irish died bungee jumping.

YOUR OPINION Write a brief paragraph expressing your opinion about why some people die and are not found for a long time. Support your opinion with evidence from the stories you have read.

_____

_____

_____

_____

_____

_____

INTO THE JUNGLE

SELECTION 1

Amazon Nightmare

Eleven-year-old Noris Villarreal was enjoying her short flight over the jungle. She had been on vacation in southeastern Venezuela, but now it was time to go back home. To get to her little village deep in the Venezuelan jungle, Noris could have traveled by canoe. But that would have taken a week. So on October 12, 1999, she boarded a small plane. It was supposed to get her home in forty-five minutes. But it didn't work out that way. In the middle of the flight, the plane's engine began to sputter. The Cesna 207 was in trouble. The pilot tried desperately to keep the plane aloft. To lighten the load, he ordered his seven passengers to toss out all their belongings. Noris, who was sitting in the last row, threw out her bags. She kept only her backpack, which contained some bread, a can of meat, and her Bible. For a few minutes it looked as if the plane might make it to the airstrip at Noris' village. But when they were still ten minutes away, the plane headed down.

The pilot tried to land the plane in the river, but missed. The Cesna crashed into trees along the riverbank. The pilot and three passengers were killed on impact. Rocio Montoya and Carlos Arteaga were badly injured. Nineteen-year-old Ismael Rodriguez suffered a gash in his head. And Noris was knocked out.

When Noris woke a couple of hours later, she felt a terrible pain in her wrist. The bones were badly broken. Still, she was relatively lucky. Rocio Montoya couldn't move, and was begging for help. Carlos Arteaga was sitting on the ground with his leg badly injured.

Noris and Ismael Rodriguez were the only ones able to walk. Ismael set off to look for help while Noris stayed with Arteaga and Montoya. Noris fed Arteaga bread from her backpack. She bandaged his wounds as best she could. She also collected water from the river and washed Montoya's face.

Hour after hour, Noris and the two others waited by the wreckage. They waited all through the night. The next morning, Ismael returned. He had not found any help. Soon he decided to try again. This time Noris went with him.

"We started to walk and walk until we got lost," Ismael later remembered. There were dense trees, bushes, and vines everywhere. All directions looked the same. As they walked, Ismael's feet began to swell up and turn purple. Noris' wrist throbbed with pain. Their bruised bodies ached. Thousands of mosquitoes and flies swarmed around them. They began to develop infections.

From time to time they wandered back to the crash site. Things looked even bleaker there. Bugs were crawling everywhere. On one return visit, they found that Rocio Montoya was missing. After complaining of thirst, she had managed to roll herself to the river. There the current had swept her away. Her body was never found. Carlos Arteaga, meanwhile, was still alive—but barely. His injuries were very bad. Noris did her best to comfort him. She brought him water and fed him the few emergency rations left from the plane.

Days passed. Noris and Ismael kept trying to find their way out of the jungle. They made no progress. Each day the heat and humidity sapped their strength. They ate fruit they found growing on trees. They drank water from jungle streams. But it wasn't enough. Malnutrition set in. So did dehydration. Each day they grew weaker. And the infections in their systems grew worse.

During the day, Noris kept her courage up. But at night she cried herself to sleep. At times she and Ismael heard search planes in the distance. But there was no way to signal them. Hidden under a deep canopy of leaves, the survivors were invisible from the air.

By October 24, Ismael was ready to give up. It had been twelve days since the crash. "I couldn't take the hunger anymore," Ismael recalled. He believed he was going to die in the jungle. Arteaga, too, was ready to die. Somehow, though, Noris kept her hope alive. She gathered plants and fed them to Ismael. She brought him more water from the river. And she prayed a lot.

The next day, Noris and Ismael again tramped through the jungle. After less than a mile, they were exhausted. They hauled themselves to the river and sat down on a rock. Again they heard search planes. Noris and Ismael didn't know it, but searchers had finally found the crash site. They had rescued Carlos Arteaga and were now combing the area for Noris and Ismael.

Four hours later, a rescue helicopter appeared over the river. Noris and Ismael waved and shouted. Noris began to cry as she realized that her nightmare in the jungle was finally ending.

It took a while for the three survivors to recover. Noris had surgery to repair her broken wrist. Ismael was treated for his cuts and infections. And Carlos Arteaga had to have his leg amputated. Still, all three were lucky to be alive.

One official described for reporters how difficult the search had been. He mentioned the tall trees and the thick vegetation. He said, "Under these conditions and because of all the days that went by, it's a true miracle to have survivors."

If you have been timed while reading this article, enter your reading time below. Then turn to the Words-per-Minute Table on page 120 and look up your reading speed (words per minute). Enter your reading speed on the graph on page 121.

Reading Time: Selection 1

_____ : _____
MINUTES   SECONDS

UNDERSTANDING IDEAS Circle the letter of the best answer.

1. Which statement belongs in the empty box?

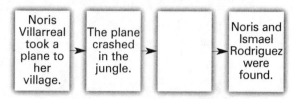

A The plane's engine began to sputter.

B Carlos Arteaga had to have his leg amputated.

C The trip to the village would take 45 minutes.

D Noris and Ismael tried to find help.

2. The pilot told passengers to throw out their belongings because

F he knew they were going to crash

G he wanted to lighten the load

H they had no parachutes

J he was sure they would make it to the airstrip

3. All of the following events were caused by the plane crash EXCEPT

A the pilot and three passengers were killed

B Noris was hungry and dehydrated

C Noris went on vacation

D Noris and Ismael tried to escape the jungle

4. Search planes couldn't find the victims because

F they had gotten into a canoe

G the search planes could only fly at night

H the dense jungle made it hard for them to see what was on the ground below

J the weather was hot and humid

SUMMARIZE For each blank, choose the word that best completes the meaning of the paragraph.

home	survived	
		rescued
successful	plane	

Noris Villarreal was trying to get

_____ the fastest way she could.

She took a small _____ on

October 12, 1999, hoping to reach her home in 45

minutes. In the middle of the flight, the plane crashed.

Four people _____ the crash, but

some of them were badly injured. During the next twelve

days, search planes tried to find them but were not

_____. Finally, as they were

about to give up all hope, Noris and the two other

survivors were _____.

IF YOU WERE THERE Write a brief paragraph explaining what you think you might do if you were stranded in the jungle after a plane crash. Be sure to include examples from the story to support your response.

_____

_____

_____

_____

_____

"They're Killing Us!"

Kevin Donaldson always flew over water. He never let his pontoon plane get more than eight miles from one of the rivers that cut through the dense Amazon forest. He figured this strategy would protect him. Even if something went wrong with his plane, he would be able to glide down and land on water. Under ordinary circumstances, Kevin's plan would have kept him safe. But April 20, 2001, was not an ordinary day.

On that morning, Kevin took off from Leticia, Colombia. Kevin had Jim and Veronica "Roni" Bowers and their two young children, Cody and Charity. Donaldson and the Bowers family were American missionaries living in Peru. For years they had lived and worked among the local people. Seven-month-old Charity was the latest addition to the Bowers family. In fact, Jim and Roni had been in Colombia doing paperwork after adopting her. Now the group was headed home.

Kevin Donaldson sat in the pilot's seat. Next to him, Jim Bowers was happily feeding Cheerios to little Charity. Roni was in the back seat with six-year-old Cody. Kevin kept the plane cruising along at 4,000 feet. Everything was going smoothly. Then Jim Bowers looked out his window and saw a strange sight. A Peruvian fighter jet was flying right below them. Knowing how much Cody loved fighter planes, Jim called out to make sure his son noticed it. Jim expected the fighter plane to pass them by quickly. But it didn't. It stayed right with them. That made Jim uneasy. He passed Charity back to Roni so he would be available in case Kevin needed his help.

Meanwhile, Kevin was radioing the control tower at their destination point in Iquitos, Peru. He wanted to know what the fighter jet was doing. He couldn't radio the jet pilot directly because the jet was using a military frequency.

Before Kevin got an answer to his question, he felt a sudden pain in his legs. At the same time, Jim heard a noise like popcorn popping. It took Jim only an instant to realize what was happening: the fighter plane was firing at them.

"Kevin!" Jim yelled. "We're being shot at!"

Kevin knew that Jim was right. "They're killing us!" he screamed to the control tower. "We're being attacked! We're being attacked!"

Indeed, the fighter plane was trying to knock them from the sky. A group of American CIA agents flying in the area had spotted Kevin's pontoon plane. They thought it belonged to drug smugglers.

So the agents had contacted the Peruvian fighter jet. Now the fighter pilot was trying to shoot the little plane down.

Ignoring the pain in his legs, Kevin attempted to guide his plane toward the Amazon River below. When the plane tilted to the left, he tried to use his foot pedals to straighten it. Then he realized he couldn't move his right leg. It had been shattered by a bullet. His left leg had also been hit.

Jim, meanwhile, grabbed the fire extinguisher and tried to put out the fire in the rear of the cabin. As the flames died down, Jim saw his wife slumped in her seat with Charity still in her lap. The baby had blood all over her face. A bullet had gone through Roni and struck Charity in the head. Both mother and child were dead.

Somehow, Kevin Donaldson managed to bring the plane down in the middle of the river. That alone was a heroic feat. But he, Jim, and Cody were not out of danger yet. Fuel was leaking from the plane. More flames sprang up around them. Jim managed to get Cody out of the cabin. The little boy was scared but unhurt. Then Jim struggled to pull out the bodies of his wife and baby daughter. He fought desperately to keep them from being swept away by the current. Kevin Donaldson also made it out of the plane. The pain in his legs was excruciating, but he ignored it and swam over to help Cody Bowers. He put the little boy on his back and swam away from the burning plane.

All this time, the fighter jet continued to pass back and forth overhead. Kevin and Jim feared it might begin shooting again at any moment. But at last it flew off.

After the fire died down, Kevin swam back to the wreck. His legs were bleeding badly. He knew he could die from loss of blood, so he used two belts and a sock to make tourniquets. He wrapped them tightly around his upper legs to slow the bleeding.

Soon local people spotted the wrecked plane. They paddled their canoes out into the river and brought everyone ashore. Then they rushed Kevin off for medical attention. He had lost so much blood that he nearly died.

The U.S. government felt bad about its part in the tragedy. So did Peru's government. But that didn't bring Roni or Charity back to life. Jim and Cody flew back to the United States with their bodies. They settled in North Carolina, where Jim's mother lived.

After undergoing surgery on both his legs, Kevin Donaldson did go back to Peru. He didn't fly a plane anymore, though. He found it too scary. The memory of his terrible ordeal was still very strong.

"It's something that will haunt me for a long time," he said.

If you have been timed while reading this article, enter your reading time below. Then turn to the Words-per-Minute Table on page 120 and look up your reading speed (words per minute). Enter your reading speed on the graph on page 121.

Reading Time: Selection 2

_____ : _____
MINUTES   SECONDS

UNDERSTANDING IDEAS Circle the letter of the best answer.

1. What were the Bowers doing on April 20, 2001?

A They were smuggling drugs.

B They were sight-seeing.

C They were getting food.

D They were going from Columbia to Peru.

2. The Peruvian jet flew close to Donaldson's plane to

F shoot it down

G give it an escort out of the country

H warn him of dangerous aircraft ahead

J help him because his engine had failed

3. Which statement belongs in the empty box?

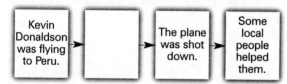

| Kevin Donaldson was flying to Peru. | | The plane was shot down. | Some local people helped them. |

A The CIA apologized.

B Kevin went back to Peru after having surgery on his legs.

C Kevin was shot in both legs.

D Jim and Cody moved to North Carolina.

4. The CIA made a terrible mistake because they

F used a Peruvian jet instead of an American jet

G shot down a plane without checking who was on board

H tried to contact Donaldson

J called the control tower in Iquitos

SUMMARIZE For each blank, choose the word that best completes the meaning of the paragraph.

nervous	pontoon	fire
fighter	killed	local

As Kevin Donaldson flew the Bowers family above the jungle, they noticed a _____ jet below them. The jet stayed right with them, which made them _____. Suddenly, the jet opened fire on the small _____ plane. Kevin was hit in both legs and Roni and Charity were _____. The plane caught _____, but somehow Kevin was able to land it on the river. Kevin, Jim, and Cody were able to get out of the plane, and some _____ people helped them.

IF YOU WERE THERE Imagine that you were piloting a small plane in the Amazon. If you saw a military jet near you, what might you do? Write a brief paragraph explaining the steps you would take. Be sure to include examples from the story to support your response.

_____

_____

_____

_____

USE CONTEXT CLUES When you read, you may find a word whose meaning is unfamiliar to you. When that happens, you can look up the word's meaning in the dictionary. You can also find out what the word means by looking for context clues. These are words or sentences that come before or after the word. Context clues can be synonyms or antonyms of the unfamiliar word. They may also be an example or definition of the unfamiliar word.

Read each excerpt from the stories you just read. Circle the letter with the best meaning of the underlined word.

1. **The pilot tried desperately to keep the plane <u>aloft</u>. To lighten the load, he ordered his seven passengers to toss out their belongings.**

   A landing

   B flying, in the air

   C heavy

   D safe, out of danger

2. **The Cesna crashed into trees along the riverbank. The pilot and three passengers were killed on <u>impact</u>.**

   F separation

   G the water

   H the runway

   J violent contact

3. **After complaining of thirst, she had managed to haul herself to the river. There the <u>current</u> had swept her away.**

   A accident

   B rescue team

   C flow of water

   D riverbank

4. **They ate fruit they found growing on trees. They drank water from jungle streams. But it wasn't enough. <u>Malnutrition</u> set in.**

   F lack of good food

   G germs from dirty water

   H tiredness

   J disease

5. **Hidden under a deep <u>canopy</u> of leaves, the survivors were invisible from the air.**

   A wall

   B covering

   C floor

   D shelter

PUT WORDS INTO CONTEXT Complete the paragraph using the underlined words from the exercise on this page.

The _____ of a plane crash in the Amazon jungle may leave a lot of debris. However, the thick _____ of the jungle trees makes it very difficult for rescuers to find survivors. Left without food for days, survivors could suffer from _____. The swift _____ of the river might make even getting a drink of water very difficult.

USING EXACT WORDS Exact words help to create a mental picture in the mind of the reader. For example, which sentence gives you a clearer image? (1) Ismael Rodriguez was hurt. (2) Nineteen-year-old Ismael Rodriguez suffered a gash to his head. Unlike Sentence 1, which creates only a general image, sentence 2 gives the reader a specific mental picture because it uses a vivid verb and descriptive words.

Read these sentences and choose the MOST exact descriptive phrase to replace the underlined words. Remember, more than one answer may make sense. Be careful to choose the MOST exact descriptive phrase.

1. **When Noris awoke, <u>she was in pain</u>.**
   A she was hurting
   B her wrist hurt
   C it was painful in her arm
   D she felt a terrible pain in her wrist

2. **As they walked, Ismael's feet <u>bothered him</u>.**
   F swelled up
   G caused throbbing, aching pain
   H hurt
   J were not normal

3. **<u>They began to develop infections</u>.**
   A They got a lot of infections.
   B Their bodies got infections.
   C Infections blossomed all over their bodies.
   D Their cuts became infected.

4. **There were <u>lots of swarming flies and mosquitoes</u>.**
   F lots of bugs
   G thousands of flies and mosquitoes swarming around them
   H lots of flies and mosquitoes in the air
   J a large number of flies and mosquitoes nearby

5. **Each day <u>the heat made it hard to go on</u>.**
   A the heat sapped their strength
   B the heat was very high
   C the heat made them weak
   D the heat was bad and caused problems

ANALOGIES As you have seen in previous exercises, analogies show relationships and patterns between words. The relationships can be very different things, not just synonyms and antonyms. For example, *hat* is to *head* as *glove* is to *hand*. The first words (*hat* and *glove*) are meant to cover the second words (*head* and *hand*). For each blank, choose an underlined word from the exercise on this page to correctly complete the analogy. **In all cases, you need only one of the words from the underlined phrase to complete the analogy.**

1. *Vultures* are to *circling* as *flies* are to

   _____ .

2. *Cold* is to *hot* as *cool* is to

   _____ .

3. *Doctor* is to *patients* as *medicine* is to

   _____ .

4. *Bruise* is to *ache* as *cut* is to

   _____ .

ORGANIZE THE FACTS To understand a passage, you should ask questions about the text before, during, and after reading, then look for answers. While you are reading, know how and where to look for answers to questions. Sometimes the answer might be stated directly in the passage; other times you need to put ideas or information together to come up with the answer. Sometimes the answer may not be in the passage at all but may be something you already know.

Look at the chart below. Then answer the questions at the right.

Question-Answer Relationships	
Question	**How to Answer**
• Where was the Bowers family going?	Question words such as *who, where,* and *when* usually indicate that the answer is right there in the passage.
• Why did the Peruvian fighter jet come so close to Donaldson's plane?	The question words *what* and *why* sometimes require you to think and to search the passage.
• Why did the fighter jet receive orders to shoot down Donaldson's plane?	A general question like this is about something you probably know. You can come up with the answer on your own.
• How do you think the fighter pilot felt after finding out that he had shot down an innocent plane?	A question that asks what you think requires you to use what you already know and what the author tells you. You will make an inference or draw a conclusion.

1. **Which question can you answer by looking for a direct statement from the story?**

    A Where were Roni and Charity Bowers when they were killed?

    B Why do you think the CIA made such a terrible mistake?

    C How did Donaldson land his plane on the river?

    D How do you think Kevin Donaldson felt when he was trying to land the plane?

2. **Which question can you answer by thinking and searching?**

    F Who was on board Donaldson's plane when it was shot down?

    G Why didn't Donaldson radio the Peruvian fighter jet?

    H How did the local people help Donaldson and the Bowers?

    J Why do you think Jim Bowers moved to North Carolina?

3. **Which question requires you to combine what you know with what the author tells you?**

    A How old was Noris when the plane crashed?

    B What were the Bowers doing in South America?

    C Why do you think Kevin Donaldson stopped flying?

    D Why did the plane crash in Venezuela?

WRITE YOUR OWN QUESTIONS Write two questions about each of the stories in this unit. For each question, explain how you would find the answer.

_____

_____

_____

_____

_____

VERIFYING EVIDENCE As a reader, it's up to you to weigh the evidence being offered in any piece of writing. When the author has written to inform or persuade, you must verify or confirm the evidence being offered and judge how believable that evidence is. Pretend you came across the following item in your daily newspaper. Read the story and then choose the best answer for each question.

[1] When a plane crashes in the ocean, the rescue mission becomes more difficult. [2] Victims have to get out of the airplane before it sinks. [3] They have to find life rafts or life vests and use them. [4] It is difficult to survive long in cold water. [5] Health experts say that hypothermia can set in quite quickly. [6] Hypothermia is a condition in which the body temperature becomes too low. [7] Another problem with ocean rescues is finding the survivors. [8] Finding a small life raft can be very hard. [9] Life rafts should carry radio transmitters and signal flares to help rescuers find survivors.

1. **Which is the best source for verifying what health experts have said?**
   A a travel magazine
   B a medical dictionary
   C the Sunday comics in a newspaper
   D the magazine *Sports Illustrated*

2. **Which fact can you verify by looking at a world atlas?**
   F the size of the major oceans
   G if modern life rafts carry signal flares
   H the definition of hypothermia
   J the difficulties of ocean rescues

3. **Which of the following offers evidence that ocean rescues are difficult?**
   A Sentences 2, 4, and 7
   B Sentences 1 and 9
   C Sentences 6 and 9
   D Sentence 9

JUDGE THE EVIDENCE To persuade the reader of an opinion or story, the author often provides evidence. It is up to the reader to judge whether the evidence presented is believable or not.

1. **Which statement supports the opinion that jungle rescues are the most difficult kind of rescues?**
   A There is plenty for a survivor to eat in the jungle.
   B Jungles have friendly animals.
   C It is difficult for rescue planes to see survivors because of dense plants and trees.
   D Swarming mosquitoes are everywhere.

2. **Which statement best supports the following opinion?**

   It is dangerous to fly in a region where drugs are being smuggled.

   F Kevin Donaldson was a very experienced pilot.
   G The CIA was shooting down planes suspected of smuggling drugs.
   H The CIA knew that drug smuggling was taking place on the river.
   J The Peruvian and American governments were working together.

PERSUADE WITH EVIDENCE Write two sentences persuading your reader that the CIA made a terrible mistake when they ordered Kevin Donaldson's plane to be shot down. Be sure to use examples from the story to support your response.

_____

_____

_____

_____

_____

SELECTION 1

Look Out Below!

"All I knew was that it was going to hurt," recalled Brendan Jones. "I blacked out before I hit the ground but landed on soft plowed fields."

Jones was an experienced skydiver. He had taken more than 3,500 jumps. On December 14, 1997, he made what he thought would be a routine jump. It turned out to be anything but routine. Jones and four other British skydivers jumped at 5,500 feet. They completed a 3,500-foot free fall holding hands. At 2,000 feet, the jumpers separated. They expected to drift away from each other as they opened their parachutes. But this time a gust of wind blew Jones into another jumper.

The chutes of the two jumpers became entangled. The other jumper jettisoned his chute. He then opened his reserve chute and floated down to safety. But Jones was still in trouble. The other jumper's chute remained caught on his. Neither chute could inflate properly. "I was stuck with the two parachutes tangled together," Jones said later. "I couldn't get free or do anything. I was just falling. I don't know how fast I was going, just painfully fast."

Jones struggled to free his chute from the other jumper's. He couldn't. At last, at about 300 feet, he deployed his reserve chute. With two uninflated chutes already over his head, it didn't help much. But it may have slowed his fall a bit. Jones hit the ground hard. Incredibly, he wasn't killed. He suffered severe bruises and a chipped vertebra. "I'm just thankful I landed on soft, plowed fields. I suppose I am lucky to be alive," he said.

Most people die when their parachutes don't inflate properly. But a few survive, usually because they hit something soft that breaks their fall. Take the case of Paul Bodey. Like Jones, he was a veteran skydiver. He had completed more than 900 jumps. In 2001, Bodey leapt out of a plane at 14,000 feet over Sydney, Australia.

At about 5,000 feet, he decided to open his chute. It malfunctioned. That sent Bodey speeding toward certain death. But just before hitting the ground, he crashed through a tree and fell onto a road. The tree cushioned Bodey's fall just enough to save him. He suffered just a punctured lung and some spinal injuries.

A flimsy corrugated iron roof saved Dave Clements. On November 11, 2000, he was skydiving at Coventry Airport in England. Skydivers use a spread-eagle position in their free falls. This position keeps them stable as they fall. But in this case, it didn't work. Somehow Clements lost control of his descent. He found himself in a wild spin, moving at well over a hundred miles per hour. "The only way I can describe it is that it was like being spun round in a tumble-dryer," said Clements.

Clements struggled to regain control of his descent. He didn't open his parachute because he feared he would become entangled in it. He couldn't tell up from down. Only at the last instant did he pull the cord to his chute. Thus, he was still going about 60 miles an hour when he crashed through the roof of an airport hangar. "I would like to say I aimed for the roof," said Clements. "But I had absolutely no control. I can't believe I'm alive. It doesn't make sense."

Paul Delaney, a British army paratrooper, can thank a muddy riverbank for saving his life. During a 1998 jump, his parachute opened properly. But the cords got tangled. He began to spin as he fell. The more he spun around, the more tangled his cords became. Tangled cords caused his chute to partly collapse. Delaney kept spinning while gaining speed. "The spinning became so violent I grew dizzy and blacked out," he said. "The next thing I knew I was on the operating table with tubes and drips and oxygen."

Delaney hit the soft riverbank at 70 miles an hour. He broke both his legs and fractured his pelvis. "It's a miracle that he survived the incident," said an army official. "He is a very lucky man to be alive."

Sometimes the softest place to land is on someone else. That happened to Kevin McIlwee, a skydiving teacher. In 2001, he jumped in tandem with his wife, Beverley, in France. He was on top and she was on the bottom. Both their main chutes and their reserve chutes failed to deploy properly. As they plunged toward the ground, Kevin said to his wife over a headset, "We might not get away with this."

But, amazingly, they did. McIlwee used all the experience of 4,500 jumps to land as softly as possible. The partially opened chutes slowed them a bit. Even so, they hit the ground with a thud. McIlwee broke his leg. But Beverley, on the bottom, took the brunt of the blow. She broke both her feet.

Dennis Murtaugh, Beverley's father, credited McIlwee's skydiving skills for saving their lives. "Kevin can drive a parachute like you can drive a car. He lands them like a feather." But then he added, "I don't think my daughter will jump again."

If you have been timed while reading this article, enter your reading time below. Then turn to the Words-per-Minute Table on page 120 and look up your reading speed (words per minute). Enter your reading speed on the graph on page 121.

Reading Time: Selection 1

_____ : _____
MINUTES   SECONDS

UNDERSTANDING IDEAS Circle the letter of the best answer.

1. **What is the main topic of all the stories in this article?**

   A skydivers that have died

   B skydivers who have survived their chutes not opening

   C what to do if your parachute doesn't open

   D how to jump out of an airplane

2. **What happens to most people when their parachutes don't inflate properly?**

   F They usually parachute again.

   G They are badly injured.

   H They don't survive.

   J They are fine.

3. **What saved Dave Clements from certain death?**

   A His parachute finally opened at 1,000 feet.

   B He hit a flimsy corrugated iron roof.

   C He hit a soft riverbank.

   D He was going 60 miles per hour.

4. **What saved the lives of Kevin and Beverly McIlwee?**

   F landing in water

   G landing in a haystack

   H communicating with headsets

   J Kevin's experience of having jumped 4,500 times

SUMMARIZE For each blank, choose the word that best completes the meaning of the paragraph.

riverbank	cushioned	alive
miracle	killed	partially

Even though you'd think that anyone would be

_____ if his or her parachute didn't

open, some have survived. Usually their parachutes

opened _____ or at the last minute. In

some cases, people's falls were _____

by a tree or the roof of a building. In another case, an

army paratrooper hit a soft _____ and

only broke his legs and pelvis. An army official said it

was a _____ he survived.

Everyone who has had this experience is amazed to be

_____.

IF YOU WERE THERE Pretend you have jumped out of an airplane and your parachute is not working properly. Write a brief paragraph explaining your reactions to this experience. Be sure to include examples from the story to support your response.

_____

_____

_____

_____

No Walk in the Park

"This will be a walk in the park," thought Dennis Butler. Twenty-six-year-old Butler was a firefighter, but in his free time he loved to climb mountains. On May 30, 2002, he planned to go up Oregon's Mount Hood. He began the trip with five other firefighters, including Assistant Fire Marshall Cleve Joiner. Joiner's 14-year-old son Cole also came along.

On May 29, the group rode a snow vehicle to 8,500 feet. At 3:45 the next morning they began climbing. They needed the early start to avoid the soft snow that develops in the warm afternoon sun. The climbers headed up a trail called the "dog route" because it is supposed to be easy enough for a dog to climb. Each year many people climb this trail. Still, it is no easy hike. Every trail on Mount Hood can be dangerous. In fact, over the past century, 130 people have died climbing this mountain. With its summit rising to 11,239 feet, Mount Hood is never "a walk in the park."

At 8:30 A.M., the group reached the Bergschrund, a crevasse just 500 feet below the summit. It consists of a deep 50-foot-long cut that runs across the face of the mountain. To get around it, the climbers divided into two groups. This part of the trail was especially steep and icy. So to be safe, the members of each group roped themselves together. Jeff Pierce, who had climbed Mount Hood a dozen times, led the first group of three. The other four came next.

Ahead of them, two other sets of climbers were making their way toward the summit. The first one consisted of four men. They were about 350 feet ahead of the firefighters. The second set, consisting of two men, was close behind the first.

One minute everyone was enjoying a beautiful climb on a beautiful day. The next minute, tragedy struck. Someone in the top group lost his footing. Like all the other climbers that morning, he was roped to his partners. So all four men began tumbling down the slope. They tried to use their ice axes and crampons on their boots to stop. But it was no use. They smacked right into the group of two men. Now six men were tumbling down the mountain.

Jeff Pierce saw them coming. He shouted, "Move right! Move right!" But he and his two companions couldn't move in time. In a flash they were hit by the full force of six falling men. A second later, they and the six others slid down the slope and vanished into the crevasse. The remaining four firefighters could only stare in horror as the disaster unfolded.

The fall into the crevasse killed three men—two from the top group and one from the second group. The other three men from the first two groups were injured. One had a broken jaw. Another had a broken pelvis, shoulder, and leg. The third had a head injury and some bad bruises. The three firefighters, meanwhile, were also hurt. Jeff Pierce suffered a deep cut on his leg. Cole Joiner hurt his back. The young man was later asked what it was like to fall into the crevasse. "It happened so quick that it was hard to think about what it was like," said Cole. "I just remember seeing climbers come down at me and then being in the hole." The third firefighter, Jeremiah Moffitt, was more seriously hurt, but at least he was still alive.

One of the four firefighters outside the crevasse called 911 on his cell phone. Soon a rescue helicopter arrived with a crew of six. The pilot fought to keep the chopper steady in the high winds and thin mountain air. Rescuers loaded two injured climbers into baskets and flew them off to safety. Then it was Jeremiah Moffit's turn. Rescue workers put him in a basket. But before he was hauled up to the helicopter, the cable went limp. For a moment no one knew what was happening. Someone must have pushed the emergency release button, but why?

The reason quickly became clear. The helicopter itself was in trouble. A gust of wind blew it against the mountain. The rotor blades sheared off when they hit rock. Rescue workers watched in horror as the crippled chopper rolled sideways a thousand feet down the mountain, flipping over about a dozen times. "Everything became dreamy and silent," said rescue worker Dave Mull. "Everything seemed to be moving in slow motion."

The rescue workers on the ground rushed down the slope. They expected to find dead bodies. Luckily, they didn't. Everyone on the helicopter had survived. One had suffered internal injuries and a broken leg and wrist. Another had a broken leg and rib. One had a neck injury. The rest walked away with just minor bruises.

Other helicopters rushed to the scene. They now had to rescue not only the climbers, but the helicopter crew. It took hours to complete the job, but at last all the survivors were safely off the mountain.

Would any of the men go climbing again? Some said they probably would. But young Cole Joiner said his experience had ended his desire to climb mountains forever. He never wanted to take another "walk in the park."

If you have been timed while reading this article, enter your reading time below. Then turn to the Words-per-Minute Table on page 120 and look up your reading speed (words per minute). Enter your reading speed on the graph on page 121.

Reading Time: Selection 2

_____ : _____
MINUTES   SECONDS

UNDERSTANDING IDEAS Circle the letter of the best answer.

1. Which statement belongs in the empty box?

| Fire-fighters set out to climb Mt. Hood. | → | They reached a huge crevasse. | → | | → | The first helicopter arrived to help. |

A They started climbing early.

B Cole Joiner doesn't want to climb again.

C Six men hit Jeff Pierce's group.

D The rescue helicopter crashed into the mountain.

2. What did the firefighters do to get around the crevasse?

F They decided to turn back.

G They divided into two groups.

H They decided to go one at a time.

J They roped together into one large group.

3. The fall into the crevasse injured many of the climbers

A and killed three of them

B but they all survived

C and killed five of them

D and left them with serious injuries

4. The only good thing about the helicopter crash was that

F the helicopter could still fly

G no one was killed

H it didn't fall very far down the mountain

J only one person was killed

SUMMARIZE For each blank, choose the word that best completes the meaning of the paragraph.

| mountains | park | |
| collision | hit | tragedy |

Before he climbed Mt. Hood, Dennis Butler thought it

would be "a walk in the _____."

He loved to climb _____. However,

the climb turned into a _____ when

some other climbers slipped on the steep ice above

them. The climbers fell down the slope and

_____ all the climbers below them.

The _____ drove nine climbers into a

deep crevasse.

IF YOU WERE THERE Imagine that you are climbing a steep, icy mountain. Someone falls and is injured. Write a brief paragraph explaining the steps you would take. Be sure to include examples from the story to support your response.

_____

_____

_____

_____

_____

_____

_____

USE CONTEXT CLUES When you read, you may find a word whose meaning is unfamiliar to you. When that happens, you can look up the word's meaning in the dictionary. You can also find out what the word means by looking for context clues. These are words or sentences that come before or after the word. Context clues can be synonyms or antonyms of the unfamiliar word. They may also be an example or definition of the unfamiliar word.

Read each excerpt from the stories you just read. Circle the letter with the best meaning of the underlined word.

1. **Jonas was an experienced skydiver. He had taken more than 3,500 jumps. On December 14, 1997, he made what he thought would be a <u>routine</u> jump.**

   A unusual because of accidents

   B regular because of repetition

   C dangerous

   D graceful

2. **Delaney kept spinning while gaining speed. "The spinning became so <u>violent</u> I grew dizzy and blacked out," he said.**

   F gentle

   G controlled

   H rough

   J high

3. **Both their main chutes and their reserve chutes failed to <u>deploy</u> properly. . . . The partially open chutes slowed them down a bit.**

   A cover

   B design or shape

   C combine

   D unfold or open

4. **At 8:30 A.M., the group reached the Bergschrund, a <u>crevasse</u> just 500 feet below the summit. It consists of a deep 50-foot-long cut that runs across the face of the mountain.**

   F hole

   G stairway

   H snowdrift

   J jump

5. **The pilot fought to keep the chopper <u>steady</u> in the high winds and thin mountain air. . . . The helicopter itself was in trouble. A gust of wind blew it against the mountain.**

   A spinning

   B drifting

   C holding still

   D landing safely

PUT WORDS INTO CONTEXT Complete the paragraph using the underlined words from the exercise on this page.

It is not uncommon for tragedy to strike when people

are doing what they think are _____

activities. Skydivers who have jumped thousands of times

may suddenly find that their chutes will not

_____ properly. Jeff Pierce and his

companions were swept into a _____

on a beautiful day climbing Mt. Hood. The

_____ fall killed some people and

injured others. Pilots tried to hold rescue helicopters

_____ while pulling the injured to

safety.

WORDS THAT COMPARE AND CONTRAST One type of context clue likens or contrasts an idea to a concept. When you see words and phrases such as *alike, different, both, also, in contrast, but*, and *yet*, you can tell that a comparison or contrast will follow.

For numbers 1 through 8, read the complete paragraph. For each numbered blank, refer to the corresponding number at the right. Choose the word that best completes the meaning of the paragraph.

The passages "Look Out Below" and "No Walk in the Park" are (1)_____ because they

(2)_____ describe accidents that were

unexpected. (3)_____, the accidents

they describe are quite (4)_____.

"Look Out Below!" describes many cases in which

skydivers have survived after their chutes have not

worked properly. (5)_____, "No Walk

in the Park" tells how climbers on Mt. Hood were injured

or killed after one person slipped high up on the peak.

(6)_____ skydiving and mountain

climbing can (7)_____ be exciting

sports, it is (8)_____ that you will be

hurt badly if you have an accident doing either activity.

1. **A** different
   B identical
   C relative
   D similar

2. **F** also
   G same
   H both
   J equal

3. **A** Similarly
   B Likewise
   C However
   D In addition

4. **F** another
   G different
   H separate
   J unlike

5. **A** Although
   B In contrast
   C Furthermore
   D In addition

6. **F** While
   G However
   H On one hand
   J In other ways

7. **A** neither
   B each
   C too
   D either

8. **F** disagree
   G likely
   H contrast
   J distinct

ORGANIZE THE FACTS The two stories you read in this unit are alike in some ways and different in other ways. A Venn diagram can show how they are alike and different. Look at the Venn diagram below. Then choose the best answer to each question.

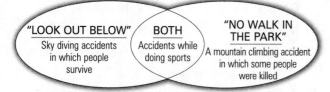

"LOOK OUT BELOW"
Sky diving accidents in which people survive

BOTH
Accidents while doing sports

"NO WALK IN THE PARK"
A mountain climbing accident in which some people were killed

1. **Which of the following belongs in the oval marked "BOTH"?**

   A It was a beautiful day on Mt. Hood.

   B Some skydivers have survived after their chutes don't open.

   C Skydiving and mountain climbing are dangerous.

   D Delaney hit the riverbank at 70 miles per hour.

2. **Which detail does NOT belong in the oval marked "Look Out Below!"?**

   F The rescue helicopter slammed into a mountain.

   G Beverly McIlwee will not jump again.

   H Accidents happen when skydivers are blown into each other.

   J Few people survive when their parachutes don't inflate properly.

3. **Which detail does NOT belong in the oval marked "No Walk in the Park"?**

   A Many people have died climbing Mt. Hood.

   B The helicopter crashed into the mountain.

   C All the survivors were safely off the mountain.

   D Dave Clements hit the roof of an airport hanger.

4. **Which detail belongs in the oval marked "No Walk in the Park"?**

   F Paul Bodey's fall was cushioned by a tree.

   G Beverly McIlwee broke both feet in a sky diving accident.

   H The helicopter's rotor blades were sheared off.

   J Tangled cords caused the parachute to collapse.

CONTINUE THE COMPARISON Fill in both of the charts below with five additional ways "Look Out Below!" and "No Walk in the Park" are alike and different.

More ways the stories are alike:
1.
2.
3.
4.
5.

More ways the stories are different:
1.
2.
3.
4.
5.

MAKE INFERENCES An author doesn't always state an idea directly in a passage, but you can often determine what the idea is by applying your own knowledge and experience. You can also examine the evidence presented in the text. This is called making an inference. Circle the letter of the best answer.

1. **What can the reader infer from the following sentences?**

> "All I knew was that it was going to hurt. I blacked out before I hit the ground but landed on soft plowed fields."

   A The person never walked again.
   B The person died in his fall.
   C The person survived his fall.
   D The person had jumped off a mountain.

2. **What can the reader infer from the first sentence of the story?**

> "This will be a walk in the park," thought Dennis Butler.

   F Butler thought something was going to be easy.
   G Butler thought something was going to be very hard.
   H Butler loved to climb mountains.
   J Butler liked to walk in parks.

3. **Which is the best inference a reader can make about this sentence?**

> Most people die when their parachutes don't inflate properly.

   A Parachuting is a very popular sport.
   B Some people survive when their parachutes don't inflate properly.
   C Parachuting is a safe sport.
   D No one survives when their parachutes don't inflate properly.

APPLY WHAT YOU KNOW Circle the letter of the best answer.

1. **What did the author intend to do in the first two paragraphs of "Look Out Below!"?**

   A make the reader curious
   B compare different skydiving techniques
   C teach a lesson about how people skydive
   D keep a record of the altitudes

2. **By saying "So to be safe, the members of each group roped themselves together," the author wanted to show that**

   F the climbers did not know what they were doing
   G the climbers were acting in a safe and responsible way
   H the climbers were behaving in a reckless manner
   J the climbers had decided not to try to cross the crevasse

JUDGE THE EVIDENCE Do you think that dangerous sports like skydiving and mountain climbing are worth pursuing? Write a brief paragraph stating your opinion. Support your position with evidence from the articles you have read.

_____

_____

_____

_____

_____

_____

Survival on a Deserted Island

Joe Rangel loved to fish. So did his buddy, Lorenzo Madrid. In the fall of 2000, these two California businessmen signed up for a week-long fishing trip in the Gulf of California. The trip took them to a remote spot thirty miles from the Baja coast. At first, they had a wonderful time. "It was Lorenzo's best trip ever," Joe later recalled. But on October 4, their happy vacation took a deadly turn.

That day, several groups of fishermen left the 90-foot boat known as "the mother ship." They set off in smaller boats to fish near some of the deserted islands in the region. Joe and Lorenzo climbed into an open boat with a young guide named José Luis Ramos Garcia. José had been on such trips before, but this time he became disoriented. He steered the boat in the wrong direction. To make matters worse, a strong wind kicked up. The little boat was blown farther and farther off course. Eventually it ran aground on the western shore of a barren island known as *Isla Angel de la Guarda*.

With darkness falling, the men realized they would have to spend the night on this island. All they had to drink were four bottles of water, three cans of beer, and one can of soda. They did have a cigarette lighter, though, so they were able to light a fire. Settling in for the night, they tried not to panic.

They hoped that in the morning the wind would die down and they could make it back to the mother ship.

The wind was a bit lighter in the morning, but a new problem arose. Their boat's motor wouldn't start. Now the men were really becoming worried. Nobody on the mother ship had any idea where they were. If they stayed in their current location, they might never be discovered. Feeling desperate, they decided to try rowing their boat north toward the mother ship. José found some driftwood to use as oars and off they went. For hours they struggled against the wind, but in the end their boat was blown back to the shore, hitting rocks and breaking up. Their cigarette lighter was lost in the crash, so they no longer had any way to start a fire.

By this time, Joe, Lorenzo, and José knew they were in serious trouble. They figured their only hope was to walk to the north end of the island, where a fishing boat was more likely to pass by. They agreed to travel along the shore in case a rescue party came along.

It was a sensible plan, but a difficult one. None of the three men was fit for the task. Like many other fishing guides, 24-year-old José had not bothered to wear shoes on this trip, so he had a tough time walking over the jagged rocks. Fifty-year-old Joe wasn't a good swimmer, so he had trouble whenever the trio needed to swim through tide pools. And 50-year-old Lorenzo was quite overweight, so he found it hard to keep moving hour after hour in the hot sun and fierce wind.

As a result, the group's progress was slow and painful. Day after day they struggled northward. They fashioned a raft from wood they found on the island. Joe and Lorenzo clung to this raft while José pulled them through the rocky tide pools. To save José's feet, Joe gave the younger man his shoes. The raft quickened their pace somewhat, but the journey remained depressingly difficult.

Meanwhile, José was doing his best to take care of the two older men. Each day he gathered food for them. Mostly their meals consisted of raw snails, sea cucumbers, and crabs. The men grew so hungry that they even ate crickets and grasshoppers. Once in a while, José spotted plastic bottles that had washed ashore. These usually contained a swallow or two of stale water or soda. It wasn't much, but the men were grateful for whatever liquid they could find.

José also found caves for them to sleep in at night. The caves were small, damp, and uncomfortable, but at least they offered some protection from the wind.

After eleven days of this, all three men were losing strength, but Lorenzo was in the worst shape of all. "He just couldn't hold on any longer," Joe later said. "He said he wanted to be in the back of the raft so we let him, and when

I turned around his face was in the water."

Joe and José scrambled to pull Lorenzo to shore. "We watched the life just go out of him," Joe recalled. "I knew what was happening. About fifteen minutes later I looked at the palms of his hands and they were blue." Joe tried to find a pulse, but couldn't. Lorenzo was dead.

Mournfully, Joe and José kept going. Two days later, having traveled a total of about twenty miles, they finally spotted a small boat belonging to commercial fishermen. Their ordeal was over! The fishermen quickly notified rescuers, who rushed to the island and picked up Joe and José. The rescuers also recovered Lorenzo's body.

José was in surprisingly good shape. He was treated at a hospital in San Felipe, Mexico, and then released. Joe Rangel had more serious problems. He had lost thirty pounds and was suffering from exposure, infection, and blood clots in his leg. Still, he knew he was lucky just to be alive.

If you have been timed while reading this article, enter your reading time below. Then turn to the Words-per-Minute Table on page 120 and look up your reading speed (words per minute). Enter your reading speed on the graph on page 121.

Reading Time: Selection 1

_____ : _____
MINUTES   SECONDS

UNDERSTANDING IDEAS Circle the letter of the best answer.

1. **Where did Joe Rangel and Lorenzo Madrid go to fish?**

   A the Atlantic Ocean

   B the Mediterranean Sea

   C near Hawaii in the Pacific Ocean

   D the Gulf of California

2. **How did the three men get stranded on the deserted island?**

   F The "mother ship" dropped them off on the island.

   G José steered their boat in the wrong direction.

   H They were blown off course by a hurricane.

   J Their small boat sank.

3. **Why did Joe, Lorenzo, and José decide to walk to the north end of the island?**

   A There was a small village there.

   B They knew they would find the "mother ship" there.

   C There would be more boats passing by the north end.

   D They would find fresh water at that end of the island.

4. **How were Joe and José finally rescued from the island?**

   F They sent a radio message.

   G A search plane spotted them.

   H The "mother ship" found them.

   J They spotted a commercial fishing boat.

SUMMARIZE For each blank, choose the word that best completes the meaning of the paragraph.

| ship | fishing | |
| island | wind | disoriented |

On October 4, 2000, Joe Rangel and Lorenzo Madrid set out in a small boat to fish. Their guide, José, became _____ and steered them in the wrong direction. A strong _____ came up, and the three men ended up on a barren island. The next day they tried to row their boat back to the mother _____ but could not due to the strong winds. They decided to walk to the north end of the _____. They thought they might find _____ boats there that would rescue them.

IF YOU WERE THERE Imagine that you were stranded on a barren island. Write a brief paragraph explaining your actions. Be sure to include examples from the story to support your response.

_____

_____

_____

_____

Clinging to Life

Janet Culver didn't know much about sailing, but her boyfriend, Nick Abbot, did. At least, Janet thought he did. Nick made money by delivering other people's sailboats to various ports. She assumed he was a careful and capable sailor. So when Nick invited Janet to come along on a trip from Bermuda to Long Island, New York, Janet leaped at the chance. She had no idea that what sounded like a romantic journey would turn into a life-and-death struggle.

The sky was blue and the breeze was light when Nick and Janet left Bermuda on the 37-foot sloop *Anaulis* on July 12, 1989. Both Nick, age 50, and Janet, age 48, were in great spirits. Nick apologized for the broken toilet on board, but Janet didn't mind. The boat didn't belong to Nick—he was just moving it to New York for its owners—and so she didn't blame him for not fixing every little thing. What she didn't know was that Nick had neglected to do other things, as well. He hadn't brought along a life raft or a shortwave radio receiver. He hadn't purchased a kit for turning salt water into drinking water. He hadn't put together an "abandon ship kit" in case of emergency. He hadn't even bothered to check the weather forecast.

Soon after they left Bermuda, they hit a storm. As the waves got bigger, Janet felt herself getting seasick. For three days and nights, they endured high waves and heavy rain. Janet's job was to steer the boat for a few hours a night so Nick could get some sleep. She managed to do it, but she was so seasick that at the end of each watch she just crawled back to bed. She wasn't able to help Nick with any of the other chores on board.

On the fourth day, the sun finally came out and Janet began to feel better. But that night something terrible happened. The wind kicked up, so Nick decided to shorten the sail. But somehow a piece of cloth became tangled in the propeller. Before Nick could sort out the problem, the propeller shaft came loose and the blade cut a big hole in the hull of the boat. Within minutes, the boat began sinking.

Now Nick's casual attitude and lack of preparation loomed large. Lacking a life raft, he and Janet had to set out in a rubber dinghy. They packed up some food from the refrigerator and grabbed some fishing gear. Then they pushed away from the boat.

"This is the worst luck anybody could have," Nick said as he and Janet watched the *Anaulis* sink.

Janet didn't think it was all bad luck. She was beginning to blame Nick for their predicament. But she hadn't been much help, either. By the time they abandoned ship, Nick was worn out. For four days he had done virtually all the work. Janet had been too seasick even to wash the dishes. Perhaps if Nick hadn't been so utterly exhausted he might have found a way to save the boat.

In any case, now the two castaways could only hope someone would come along and rescue them. Day after day, they drifted in the little dinghy. Initially they were drenched by rain. Later they were burned by the sun. With water constantly splashing into the dinghy, their clothes stayed wet. The saltwater rubbed against their skin, causing hideous sores. They had only a half gallon of fresh water, so as the days passed they became thirstier and thirstier. Nick fashioned a spear gun from some of the fishing equipment. He managed to catch one fish about the size of a flounder. But it wasn't enough. Soon they weren't just thirsty; they were also terribly hungry.

By the tenth day, Nick couldn't take it anymore. "Life isn't worth living like this," he told Janet. "I'm so sore and thirsty that I can't go on. There's no point." With that, he tumbled into the water and began swimming away from the dinghy. As Janet watched, his head slumped forward into the water and he disappeared beneath the waves.

Now Janet was all alone. She hung on another day, then another and another. At one point it rained and she managed to collect some of the rainwater to drink. Still, she knew time was running out.

"My sores were really getting bad, all open and swollen and very painful," she later recalled. "I used to be strong—5 feet 5 inches and 130-some pounds. Now I was this puny, bony creature slumped at one end of the [dinghy], wishing a fish would jump in."

At last, on July 30, a research boat called *Geronimo* passed close to the dinghy. By this time Janet had been adrift for fourteen days and was more dead than alive. She barely had the energy left to signal the passing boat. She just grabbed an orange life-vest and waved it feebly in the air. Luckily, someone on board the *Geronimo* noticed it and the crew rushed to her rescue.

When Janet arrived at the hospital, she was severely dehydrated and in desperate need of skin grafts on her feet and buttocks. She spent weeks recuperating before returning to her New Jersey home. By then, she had come to terms with Nick's death. But she would never forget the difficult lesson she had learned. As she put it, "ignorance and stupidity don't pay at sea."

If you have been timed while reading this article, enter your reading time below. Then turn to the Words-per-Minute Table on page 120 and look up your reading speed (words per minute). Enter your reading speed on the graph on page 121.

Reading Time: Selection 2

_____ : _____
MINUTES   SECONDS

UNDERSTANDING IDEAS Circle the letter of the best answer.

1. **How did Nick Abbot make money?**

   A He delivered sailboats to various ports.

   B He raced sailboats.

   C He bought and sold sailboats.

   D He worked as a crew member.

2. **Which of the following were things that Nick neglected?**

   F He didn't have a life raft.

   G He didn't have a kit for turning salt water into drinking water.

   H He hadn't put together an "abandon ship kit."

   J All of the above

3. **When the propeller shaft came loose,**

   A the blade cut a hole in the hull of the boat

   B it tore the sail

   C the propeller floated away

   D Nick was able to fix it

4. **Why didn't Janet think it was all bad luck when the boat sank?**

   F She thought Nick was a bad businessman.

   G She realized Nick had not prepared for an emergency.

   H She thought the sea wasn't dangerous.

   J She had always thought that luck did not count for much.

SUMMARIZE For each blank, choose the word that best completes the meaning of the paragraph.

seasick	storm
boat	rain
	weather

When Janet and Nick left Bermuda, the sun was shining. Unfortunately, Nick had not bothered to check the _____ forecast. Soon after they left Bermuda, they hit a big _____. For three days and nights they had heavy winds, waves, and _____. Janet became terribly _____ and spent most of the time in bed. Nick had to take care of almost everything on the _____.

IF YOU WERE THERE Write a brief paragraph explaining what you would do if you were floating on a dinghy after a shipwreck. Be sure to include examples from the story to support your response.

_____

_____

_____

_____

_____

USE CONTEXT CLUES When you read, you may find a word whose meaning is unfamiliar to you. When that happens, you can look up the word's meaning in the dictionary. You can also find out what the word means by looking for context clues. These are words or sentences that come before or after the word. Context clues can be synonyms or antonyms of the unfamiliar word. They may also be an example or definition of the unfamiliar word.

Read each excerpt from the stories you just read. Circle the letter with the best meaning of the underlined word.

1. **José had been on such trips before, but this time he became <u>disoriented</u>. He steered the boat in the wrong direction.**

   A arrogant

   B careless

   C confused

   D tired

2. **They hoped the wind would die down. . . . The wind was a bit <u>lighter</u> in the morning, but a new problem arose.**

   F less dark

   G stronger

   H gusty

   J less strong

3. **They figured their only hope was to walk to the north end of the island. . . . They agreed to travel along the <u>shore</u> in case a rescue party came along.**

   A coast

   B prop

   C support

   D mountain

4. **As a result, the group's progress was slow and painful. . . . The raft quickened their <u>pace</u> somewhat, but the journey remained depressingly difficult.**

   F problem

   G speed

   H pleasure

   J weariness

5. **José was in surprisingly good shape. He was treated at a hospital in San Felipe, Mexico, and then <u>released</u>.**

   A kept in the hospital

   B allowed to leave

   C told to come back

   D given more treatments

PUT WORDS INTO CONTEXT Complete the paragraph using the underlined words from the exercise on this page.

Joe Rangel and Lorenzo Madrid were on a fishing trip. Everything was going well until their guide, José, became

_____ and the three were lost. They

landed on the _____ of a remote

island. They began walking to the north end where they

had a better chance of being rescued, but their

_____ was slow. Lorenzo died,

Joe had serious problems, but José was

_____ from the hospital quickly.

SUFFIXES A suffix is one or more letters added to the end of a word to change its meaning. For example, the suffix *–dom* means "a state of being." So when you add the suffix *–dom* to the end of the word *free*, you get *freedom*, which means "the state of being free."

Use a dictionary to find the meaning of each suffix below. Match the suffix with its meaning on the right. Examples for each definition are included in italics. Write the letter of the correct definition on the line.

_____ **1.** -able

_____ **2.** -ous

_____ **3.** -ize

_____ **4.** -tion

_____ **5.** -al

_____ **6.** -ward

_____ **7.** -er

A pertaining to, characterized by: *fictional*

B make like, be like: *criticize*

C action, state of: *ambition*

D can be acted upon: *breakable*

E in the direction of: *backward*

F full of, having the qualities of: *generous*

G one who, a person who: *player*

WRITE DEFINITIONS Underline the suffix and write the definition of the word on the line provided.

1. realize

definition: _____

2. poisonous

definition: _____

3. changeable

definition: _____

4. northward

definition: _____

5. direction

definition: _____

6. reporter

definition: _____

7. betrayal

definition: _____

FIND THE PURPOSE Authors write to inform or teach, to persuade or convince, or to entertain. Many times authors write for more than one purpose. Advertisements, for example, can fit all three purposes for writing. The ad may inform you about a product or service you can buy. It attempts to persuade you to buy it, and it may be entertaining so that it appeals readily to a large number of people. Read the chart below. Then answer the questions.

AUTHOR'S PURPOSE		
to inform (teach)	**to persuade (convince)**	**to entertain (amuse)**
• teach history, science, and other subjects	• argue for or against an issue	• appeal to a reader's interest
• report an event	• convince people to buy	• make people laugh
• explain a process	• tell people how to act	• tell a personal story
• describe facts	• editorial appearing in a newspaper	• put words together in a poem

1. **What would be the primary purpose of a TV comedy about survival on a desert island?**

   A to inform

   B to persuade

   C to entertain

   D all of the above

2. **What would be the purpose of Janet Culver writing an editorial to a newspaper about safety at sea?**

   F to inform

   G to persuade

   H to entertain

   J all of the above

3. **What was Janet Culver's purpose when she said, "Ignorance and stupidity don't pay at sea"?**

   A to inform

   B to persuade

   C to entertain

   D all of the above

4. **What would be the purpose of a humorous play designed to promote safety at sea?**

   F to inform

   G to persuade

   H to entertain

   J all of the above

WRITE WITH A PURPOSE Write a topic sentence about being prepared when going to sea for each of the purposes you reviewed in this lesson.

to inform: _____

_____

to persuade: _____

_____

to entertain: _____

_____

MAKE PREDICTIONS You can make predictions, or educated guesses, based on what you already know. For instance, if you know that a store sells supplies for sailboats, you can reasonably predict that they would have the items you would want to have if you had to abandon ship.

Read this passage, and answer the following questions based on what you know after reading the stories in this unit.

Abandon Ship!

There are important things that any sailor should have on a boat in case of an emergency. Two of these items are a fire extinguisher and a life raft. The life raft should be easy to get to. It should contain food supplies and a kit for turning salt water into fresh water. It should also carry signal flares, waterproof matches, a flashlight, first aid kit, and a two-way radio. Remember, the life raft and what is in it can save your life!

---

1. **What do you predict sailors might do after reading the passage above?**

   A get emergency supplies

   B ignore the advice

   C sell their boats

   D repaint their boats

2. **What do you predict a good sailor would do if a storm was coming?**

   F ignore the weather report

   G set sail immediately

   H put off the trip until the storm had passed

   J buy a new flag

3. **If you were waiting to be rescued, what item would you want to use first?**

   A a two-way radio

   B waterproof matches

   C a fire extinguisher

   D food supplies

JUDGE THE BASIS OF A PREDICTION For predictions to be reasonably accurate, they must be based on what you know to be factual information. Choose the best answer.

1. **What statement helps you predict that having the right emergency equipment saves lives?**

   A Carrying emergency supplies is not necessary.

   B Signal flares are a good item to carry on a boat.

   C Remember, the life raft and what is in it can save your life.

   D The life raft should be easy to get to.

2. **Which new information helps predict that some sailors go to sea prepared?**

   F a survey that lists emergency supplies sailors carry

   G a survey of current sailboat prices

   H a map showing the location of sunken sailboats

   J a map of popular routes taken by sailboats

PREDICT WHAT YOU WOULD DO Write a brief paragraph explaining what you predict are the steps you would take before going on a long voyage. Use examples from the stories you have just read to explain your actions.

_____

_____

_____

_____

_____

_____

SELECTION 1

In Over Their Heads

"It wasn't that bad at first," said Rebecca Welch.

That's what most of the twenty-one firefighters thought as they headed into a canyon along the Chewuch River to fight a fire on July 10, 2001. The fire was called "Thirtymile Fire" because it broke out near Thirtymile Campground in Washington's Cascade Mountains. Many of the firefighters were rookies. Twenty-two-year-old Welch, for instance, had just graduated from college; this was only her second fire.

The fire had already consumed about 5,000 acres of forest, but by July tenth it seemed largely under control. Welch and the others were just supposed to work on a few smoldering acres on the south side of the river. All morning they dug fire lines to keep the flames from spreading. It was hot, difficult work, and by 2:00 P.M. it was clear they weren't having much success. Welch's squad leader, Tom Craven, reported that the fire had jumped across the fire lines from treetop to treetop. The fire was now on two sides of them. It was time to pull out before someone got hurt.

Welch, Craven, and the others did pull back. They went to a designated "safe zone," where they relaxed and ate lunch. Rebecca Welch even took a nap.

Then they were instructed to move to the north side of the river to fight another branch of the blaze.

As they worked there, the fire suddenly exploded. It began burning out of control, quickly covering 2500 fresh acres. Welch didn't know exactly what was happening, but she heard Tom Craven say, "It's time to get out right now. Right now."

Seven of the firefighters scrambled into a van and drove off. They just made it to safety before the flames cut off their escape route. The other fourteen, including Welch and Craven, were not so lucky. Their van couldn't get through, so they turned around and took off in the other direction, stopping at a place that seemed relatively safe. At least here they couldn't see any flames. As they pondered their next move, two campers drove up. Bruce and Paula Hegmeyer had been camping in the woods and now they, too, were trying to get out. As they talked to the firefighters, they heard a noise rising behind them.

"It was like the sound of a freight train," Welch recalled.

The fire came racing over the ridge, directly toward them.

"It was roaring," said Welch. "It was eating things up." Welch knew that thunderstorms were predicted for later that day, and she had the sudden thought that rain might save them. She wished the skies would open up and dampen the fire. Amazingly enough, at that moment she did feel rain start to fall. Her heart leapt with hope, but then she realized these weren't raindrops at all. As she later put it, "It was raining embers."

Welch, Craven, and the other twelve firefighters knew what they had to do. It was time to deploy their "shake and bake" kits. These were single-person tents made of aluminum and fiberglass. The tents were really more like blankets and they were the last resort of every firefighter. If a person climbed inside and sealed down the edges, he or she could survive temperatures up to 600 degrees F.

Craven and a few others set up their tents on a rocky slope. The rest, including Welch, found flatter ground. As Welch opened her kit, however, she heard the Hegmeyers crying out, "Help us, help us."

That's when Rebecca Welch became a hero.

She knew her tent could only hold one person. It might be possible to squeeze in a second person, but fitting in a third was unimaginable. Nonetheless, Welch directed Paula and Bruce to curl up inside her tent. Then she tried to crawl in on top. She didn't quite make it. Her right side stuck out. Desperately, she pulled her shirt up over her face and tried to hold it in place with a gloved hand. Then she began to pray.

It seemed to Welch that she and the Hegmeyers were huddled together for an eternity, but it was really only about five minutes. The fire roared over them, then moved on. Soon they heard a fellow firefighter calling everyone to the river, so they stood up and ran over the blackened ground, flinging themselves into the water. After the intense heat of the fire, the water was numbingly cold.

The immediate danger had passed, but the damage was unbelievable. The whole area had been burned black. Welch had second-degree burns on her right side where the flames had licked at her. Firefighter Jason Emhoff was in even worse shape. More than 25 percent of his body had been burned, and charred flesh was now dripping from his hands. Worst of all, Tom Craven and three others who had set up their tents on the rocky slope were dead. They hadn't been able to seal off their tents on the uneven rocks. The hot gases from the fire had gotten in and asphyxiated them.

As word of the disaster spread, people everywhere expressed sympathy and admiration for the victims and survivors of the fire. No one, however, was more appreciative than Paula and Bruce Hegmeyer. They knew they owed their lives to Rebecca Welch.

If you have been timed while reading this article, enter your reading time below. Then turn to the Words-per-Minute Table on page 120 and look up your reading speed (words per minute). Enter your reading speed on the graph on page 121.

Reading Time: Selection 1

_____ : _____
MINUTES   SECONDS

UNDERSTANDING IDEAS Circle the letter of the best answer.

1. Which picture BEST describes what "In Over Their Heads" is about?

1 forest fire   **2** scuba diver

3 a tiger   **4** a huge wave

A Picture 1

B Picture 2

C Picture 3

D Picture 4

2. What happened after everyone moved to what they thought was a safe area?

F Everyone began digging fire lines.

G The fire came racing over the ridge.

H They were able to escape the fire in their van.

J They moved to the river.

3. How did Rebecca Welch save the Hagmeyers' lives?

A She gave fire tents to each of them.

C She gave them driving directions.

B She helped them get into the river.

D She shared her one-person fire tent with them.

4. Tom Craven died in the fire because

F he did not have a fire tent

G his fire tent was on uneven ground

H he tried to outrun the fire

J he shared a tent with several people

SUMMARIZE For each blank, choose the word that best completes the meaning of the paragraph.

trapped	exploded	control
afternoon	river	smoldering

On July 10, 2001, the Thirtymile Fire seemed largely

under _____. Rebecca Welch and

other members of her crew were working on a few

_____ acres. However, during the

_____ the fire had jumped across their

lines. After pulling back, they were sent to another area

on the north side of the _____. After

they got there, the fire suddenly _____.

Some of the firefighters escaped, but the rest were

_____ with no way to get out.

IF YOU WERE THERE Write a brief paragraph explaining what you would do if your best friend decided to be a firefighter. Be sure to include examples from the story to support your response.

_____

_____

_____

_____

_____

Townhouse Tragedy

The call came shortly after midnight on May 30, 1999. A townhouse in northeast Washington, D.C., was on fire. "It was just an ordinary, routine fire," said firefighter Kwame Roberts. But as Battalion Chief Damian Wilk would later say, "It's the routine fires that get you."

Engine 26 was the first truck on the scene. Firefighters Joe Morgan and Louis Matthews didn't hesitate. Matthews had seven years' experience in fighting fires and Morgan had eight, so they knew what they were doing. They moved quickly to lay out the hose and attach it to a nearby hydrant. Then they entered the smoke-filled building. Charles Redding, a seventeen-year veteran of the force, was right behind them.

There were no reports of people trapped inside the house. In fact, the owners had run outside after the smoke alarm woke them up. But firefighters don't take anything for granted. It is standard procedure to make sure no one is caught inside a burning building. And so the men made their way through thick black smoke in search of inhabitants.

"We couldn't see anything, no fires showing anywhere," remembered Redding.

Soon other firefighters joined them. Engine 10 arrived, bringing more firefighters and hoses into the building. In all, twenty men were in there, all trying to find and extinguish the blaze.

Anthony Phillips, a firefighter with four years' experience, felt his way to the top of the basement stairs. There were some flames there. Firefighters trained their hoses on them. That seemed to bring them under control, and it looked as though the worst might be over. But in fact the worst was yet to come.

"After we put out that fire, the heat became real intense," said Redding.

The men didn't know it, but heat was building down in the basement. That's where the fire had started. It had been caused by an electrical problem. The air in the basement was reaching astronomically high temperatures, perhaps as high as 2,000 degrees Fahrenheit. Suddenly this super-heated air came billowing up the stairs, filling the house with deadly gases and flames.

"I had never been in a fire that hot in my life," said Redding. "The heat was just coming through our clothes. . . . It was like the fire was on our skin."

Phillips, at the head of the stairs, was in the worst position. The heat knocked him over and he fell, unconscious, on the spot. Morgan and Matthews, who were right behind him, didn't fall but they did drop their hose. Morgan called out to Matthews, and the two of them scrambled wildly to find it. The dense smoke and unbearable heat made it hard to move, but at last Morgan found the hose. He and Matthews crawled desperately along the hose toward the front door.

Outside, Chief Wilk sensed that things were turning bad. He gave the order for everyone to evacuate the building. So all of the other firefighters also turned and headed out of the townhouse.

Most of them made it. In fact, more than a dozen exited without injury. But five were not so lucky. Stanley Taper inhaled so much smoke that he required medical attention. Charles Redding suffered burns on his face and the lower part of his body. He ended up in the hospital, where doctors listed him in serious condition.

That left three firefighters still inside the burning building. Wilk sent eight men in to find them. The men found Joe Morgan and Louis Matthews struggling toward the door, both barely conscious. Quickly the other men pulled them the rest of the way out. Morgan was in bad shape. More than 60 percent of his body was burned. He was rushed to the hospital in critical condition. Doctors gave him only a 50-50 chance of surviving.

Matthews was also in critical condition. He had third-degree burns over 90 percent of his body. Doctors kept him alive for several hours, but at 2:45 that afternoon, Louis Matthews died.

Anthony Phillips was the last one brought out of the fire. He was still unconscious. In fact, he was barely alive. Rescue workers did their best, but he died less than an hour later.

Throughout the city, people mourned the loss of Matthews and Phillips. They also prayed for Joe Morgan. As the hours passed, Morgan did finally stabilize. Still, his body was swelled up almost beyond recognition. He was on a respirator for almost a month. Over the next year, he had twenty operations to repair the damage to his skin. And throughout his long recovery, he suffered excruciating pain.

Despite it all, Joe Morgan remained modest and upbeat. "I was just a guy doing his job," he said. Reflecting on his survival, he added, "I think I beat the odds."

If you have been timed while reading this article, enter your reading time below. Then turn to the Words-per-Minute Table on page 120 and look up your reading speed (words per minute). Enter your reading speed on the graph on page 121.

Reading Time: Selection 2

_____ : _____
MINUTES   SECONDS

UNDERSTANDING IDEAS Circle the letter of the best answer.

1. **Heat was building in what part of the house?**
   A the kitchen
   B the basement
   C the attic
   D the walls

2. **The fire on May 30, 1999, was caused by**
   F a gas problem
   H an electrical problem
   G someone playing with matches
   J a person who set the fire on purpose

3. **How did two firefighters use their hose?**
   A They used it to put out the fire.
   B They used it to find their way out of the building.
   C They used it to reduce the heat where they were.
   D They were not able to use their hose.

4. **When Chief Wilk said, "It's the routine fires that get you," he meant**
   F no one expects them to be dangerous, but they are
   G there are few dangerous fires
   H all fires are routine fires
   J the firefighters were not prepared

SUMMARIZE For each blank, choose the word that best completes the meaning of the paragraph.

| twenty | hose | hesitate |
| deadly | escaped | hot |

When Joe Morgan and Louis Matthews arrived at the fire, they did not _____. They laid out their _____ and then entered the smoke-filled building. It seemed that everyone had _____, but they wanted to be sure. They were joined by other firefighters, bringing the total number inside to _____. Suddenly the fire became incredibly _____. The intense heat and _____ gases drove the firefighters out and two were killed.

IF YOU WERE THERE Write a paragraph explaining what you would do if you had to go into a burning building to rescue a fellow firefighter. Be sure to include examples from the story to support your response.

_____

_____

_____

_____

_____

USE CONTEXT CLUES When you read, you may find a word whose meaning is unfamiliar to you. When that happens, you can look up the word's meaning in the dictionary. You can also find out what the word means by looking for context clues. These are words or sentences that come before or after the word. Context clues can be synonyms or antonyms of the unfamiliar word. They may also be an example or definition of the unfamiliar word.

Read each excerpt from the stories you just read. Circle the letter with the best meaning of the underlined word.

1. **That's what most of the 21 firefighters thought as they headed into a canyon along the Chuwuch River on July 10, 2001.**
   A went
   B ran
   C jogged
   D moved quietly

2. **The fire had already consumed 5,000 acres of forest, but by July 10, it seemed largely under control.**
   F exhausted
   G drained
   H burned up
   J opened

3. **Craven and a few others set up tents on a rocky slope. The rest, including Welch, found flatter ground.**
   A riverbank
   B hill
   C valley
   D cave

4. **He gave the order to evacuate the building. . . . Most of them made it. In fact, more than a dozen exited without injury.**
   F destroy
   G leave
   H cover
   J hose

5. **It seemed to Welch that she and the Hegmeyers were huddled together for an eternity, but it was really only about five minutes.**
   A a very long time
   B a universe
   C a cosmos
   D a very short time

PUT WORDS INTO CONTEXT Complete the paragraph using the underlined words from the exercise on this page.

When the firefighters _____ into the fire zone, they had no idea what was going to happen. They did not realize that they were near the center of the fire that had already _____ 5,000 acres. Suddenly, the fire was upon them. They had to set up their fire tents, some on a rocky _____. After what seemed like an _____, the fire passed and most of them survived.

GREEK AND LATIN ROOTS As you have learned, one way of finding out the meaning of a word is by looking for its root. If you know the meaning of a root word, you can often decipher the meaning of a word you don't know. Many words we use in English have Latin and Greek roots. The chart below shows some examples.

Root	Origin	Meaning	Examples
dic	Latin	say, speak	diction, predicted, dictated
habit	Latin	to have, to hold	habitat, inhabitants, inhabit
sign	Latin	sign	signal, designate, significant
mono	Greek	one	monopolize, monotone, monoxide
phys	Latin	medicine	physical, physician

For numbers 1 through 6, read the complete paragraph. For each numbered blank, refer to the corresponding question number. Choose a word from the chart that best completes the meaning of the paragraph.

The (1)_____ of rural

mountain areas in California worry about forest fires in

the summer and fall. For years, fire officials have

(2)_____ that because of dry

conditions there was a danger of fires. They

(3)_____ particular areas as

having an extreme fire danger. Often fires are started by

lightning or careless campers. Firefighters often cannot

get close to the main part of a big blaze. Many who have

tried have been seriously injured and needed to go to a

(4)_____ for treatment. They may

have suffered burns, or they may have been poisoned by

carbon (5)_____ gases.

1. **A** physical
   B signal
   C habitat
   D inhabitants

2. **F** predicted
   G dictated
   H monotone
   J physician

3. **A** diction
   B designate
   C physician
   D monopolize

4. **F** decimal
   G physical
   H signal
   J physician

5. **A** designate
   B physical
   C monoxide
   D signal

ORGANIZE THE FACTS

ORGANIZE THE FACTS There are several different ways to organize your writing. In stories like the ones you just read, the causes (why things happen) and the effects (what happens as a result) are very important. Complete the chart below with the correct cause or effect.

Cause	Effect
The air temperature in the basement was reaching as high as 2000 degrees Fahrenheit.	
	Chief Wilk ordered everyone to evacuate the building.
Three firefighters were still inside the building.	
	Anthony Phillips died less than an hour after being brought out of the building.
Joe Morgan had twenty operations to repair the damage to his skin.	

ANSWER CAUSE-AND-EFFECT QUESTIONS Choose the best answer for each question.

1. **What effect could result from being in the wrong place in a forest fire?**

   A death

   B time

   C cheer

   D warning

2. **Why did the following events happen?**

   > Tom Craven and others were killed in a Washington state forest fire, and Anthony Phillips and Louis Matthews were killed in a building in Washington, D.C.

   F They were all trained poorly.

   G They were inexperienced at their jobs.

   H They were on vacation.

   J They were in dangerous situations without realizing it.

MAKE YOUR OWN CAUSE-AND-EFFECT CHART Choose another dangerous job and fill in the chart.

Cause	Effect

FACT AND OPINION Facts and opinions can sometimes be hard to tell apart. To tell if something is a fact or an opinion, determine whether it can be proven to be true. If it can, it's a fact. If it states what someone thinks or how someone feels, it's an opinion. Read this passage, then circle the best answer to each question.

[1] The Eagle River Fire Protection Department in Colorado operates the best training program in the state. [2] The students seem to enjoy working with engineers, lieutenants, firefighters, and a battalion chief. [3] They are able to experience first-hand what it's like to contain a fire. [4] The department services an area that is approximately 65 square miles, plus thousands of acres adjacent to the White River National Forest.

1. **Which sentence from the paragraph states a FACT about the size of the area the department serves?**

   A Sentence 1

   B Sentence 2

   C Sentence 3

   D Sentence 4

2. **Which sentence from the paragraph states an OPINION about the program's reputation?**

   F Sentence 1

   G Sentence 2

   H Sentence 3

   J Sentence 4

JUDGE THE EVIDENCE Think back to the stories you have read. Review the paragraph at the left. Then choose the best answer.

1. **Which of the following statements is TRUE?**

   A Firefighting does not require special skills.

   B Most people who become firefighters die early.

   C Firefighters get injured in fires that go out of control.

   D Student firefighters learn only from routine fires.

2. **Which of the following statements is FALSE?**

   F Fire tents protect firefighters.

   G Even a small fire can cause serious problems.

   H Routine fires should not be taken seriously.

   J Student firefighters must learn special skills.

YOUR OPINION Write a brief paragraph expressing your opinion about being a firefighter. Support your opinion with evidence from the stories you have read.

_____

_____

_____

_____

_____

_____

Miracle in a Tree

The flood caught Carolina Pedro by surprise. On February 27, 2000, she was picking vegetables in the fields of Mondiano, a small village in Mozambique. "It was Sunday afternoon about four o'clock and the waters began rising," she said. "The water was coming right up to the house and was getting stronger and stronger, so, like everyone else in the village, we headed for the trees."

Because the floodwaters rose so fast, Carolina did not have time to take any food or drinking water. She just ran with her two small children to a large tree. "I did not have the time to think about anything. I just wanted to be safe," she said.

Carolina lifted her children onto a branch. Somehow she also managed to pull herself up. Normally this would not have been difficult. But Carolina was nine months pregnant. Her baby was due any day. As she climbed higher into the tree, she thought of her husband, Salvador. He was off working in the capital city of Maputo. She hoped she and the children would live to see him again.

All together, fifteen villagers sought refuge in the same tree. They waited for the waters to drop. But that didn't happen. Instead, the waters grew steadily higher. Heavy rains and a recent cyclone combined to create the worst flood in southern Africa in more than a hundred years. No one could remember seeing the country's fifteen rivers rise so fast or spread so far beyond their banks. Rivers that had been little more than a trickle quickly grew to be two miles wide. Thousands of cattle were lost in the flood. A quarter of the crops were wiped out. More than 700 people drowned and over a million were left homeless. As one man put it, "We are a country abandoned by God."

Carolina and her children stayed in the tree for three long days. It was sheer misery. No one had any food or water. "We had nothing to eat," said Carolina, "and the children cried and cried, but we could do nothing for them."

Carolina knew that if she fell asleep, she might easily roll off the branch and drown in the raging waters below. That is just what happened to one old woman from the village. As the hours passed, the woman grew weaker and weaker. At last she lost her grip on the tree. She fell into the water and was swept away.

During the day, Carolina and the others baked in temperatures of more than 100 degrees. Night brought no relief. That was when swarms of mosquitoes came out. There were other creatures to worry about as well. Many animals had crawled up the tree to escape the flood. These included rats, stinging ants, and snakes.

As Carolina clung to the tree, rescue efforts were launched to save flood victims. Volunteers from several nations came to the aid of thousands of people who were trapped on rooftops or in trees. At last, on March 1, a South African helicopter arrived over the tree in Mondiano. The chopper hovered overhead as the crew began lifting people to safety. Carolina was barely aware of what was happening. "I was feeling a lot of pain since I spent three days without eating anything," she said. "I was hungry and thirsty and tired." Beyond that, she was now in labor. Her baby was about to be born. When pilot Chris Berlyn saw this, he quickly flew back to his base camp and picked up a medic. But by the time the medic arrived, Carolina had already given birth to a healthy baby girl. The helicopter crew pulled Carolina and the baby to safety. Everyone in the tree was saved.

The rescue was caught on film and broadcast around the world. The little girl, named Rositha, was called a "miracle baby" or "tree baby." In a sea of death and destruction, people saw her as a symbol of hope. People from around the world sent money and clothes to her and her family.

Rositha's father was thrilled to learn that his wife was safe and that he had a new baby daughter. He was also pleased by the media's coverage of the rescue. He hoped it would help everyone realize what his people had been through during this terrible flood. "We are very happy that these pictures were seen around the world," he said. "It means that the world understands what happened to the people of Mozambique."

If you have been timed while reading this article, enter your reading time below. Then turn to the Words-per-Minute Table on page 120 and look up your reading speed (words per minute). Enter your reading speed on the graph on page 121.

Reading Time: Selection 1

_____ : _____
MINUTES   SECONDS

UNDERSTANDING IDEAS Circle the letter of the best answer.

1. **Why was it difficult for Carolina Pedro to climb the tree?**

   A She was nine months pregnant.

   B She had a broken leg.

   C She was tired.

   D She almost drowned.

2. **The animals that had crawled up in the tree with the villagers included**

   F dogs, cats, and snakes

   G stinging ants, a jaguar, and a dog

   H rats, stinging ants, and snakes

   J snakes, bats, and cats

3. **Which of the following statements is FALSE?**

   A Carolina had her baby in the tree.

   B Carolina had her baby in the helicopter.

   C Carolina and her children were saved from the flood.

   D Carolina's baby was called the "miracle baby."

4. **What did Carolina's husband say about the media coverage?**

   F He did not like the publicity.

   G He wished the media had not bothered local people.

   H He thought they did a very bad job telling the story.

   J He was glad the world would know what happened.

SUMMARIZE For each blank, choose the word that best completes the meaning of the paragraph.

birth	trees	
waters	children	baby

On February 27, 2000, Carolina Pedro noticed that the

_____ were rising fast next to her

village in Mozambique. She and her neighbors fled

quickly to _____. She took her two

small _____ with her. It was hard for

her to pull herself up because she was about to

have a _____. Carolina gave

_____ to her new daughter before

rescuers pulled them from the trees.

IF YOU WERE THERE Imagine that you are staying up in the tree next to Carolina Pedro. Write a brief paragraph explaining what you would do in order to stay alive. Be sure to include examples from the story to support your response.

_____

_____

_____

_____

_____

_____

Tragic Mudslide

When Joanna Saavedra saw the floodwaters rising outside her home in northern Venezuela, she knew she had to get away fast. She picked up her three-year-old son and stepped outside. But as soon as she did, the raging waters swept her off her feet. "The massive water was so strong," she said.

Somehow Saavedra managed to grab hold of a tree branch. She pulled herself and her son up out of the swirling flood. For thirty long minutes the two of them clung to that tree. Saavedra knew that when the rising water reached them, they would both die. But suddenly a man appeared in a boat. He was a local firefighter searching for survivors. He rescued Saavedra and her son from the tree and took them to a local school that was serving as a makeshift shelter. Said Saavedra gratefully, "The fireman made miracles happen."

Saavedra's story was one of the very few happy ones in Venezuela in mid-December 1999. That's when torrential rains hit the northern coast along the Caribbean Sea. The rain lasted for days, causing huge floods in the region. The heavy rains loosened the soil on the steep hills along the coast. That spelled disaster for the many thousands of Venezuelans who lived in shantytowns there.

On December 15, the highly saturated soil on the hills simply gave way. Huge avalanches of mud washed away countless shanties. The mud swept away the home of José Laya. "I have lived through one earthquake and other terrible things," he said, "but nothing in my life has compared to this. I will never forget the loud roar that the floods made. You can never forget something so savage."

Once the land gave way, there was no stopping the mud until it reached the sea. The mud knocked down trees with trunks the diameter of manhole covers. It dislodged rocks reported to be the size of small cars. After destroying the shanties, it plowed into high-rise apartment buildings. Finally, mud and debris crashed through the fancy hotels that dotted the beach.

Some people refused to leave their homes until the last possible moment. Dania Milano and her family stayed for three days, watching and waiting. At last they heard the unmistakable sound of mud rushing toward them. Milano gathered up her children and ran down the hill to safety. She looked back just as a giant wave of mud split her house in two. "The mountain came down and the walls of our house broke," she said. "We lost everything. The house opened into two parts."

For the survivors, losing their homes was only the beginning of the misery. They also had to deal with the loss of loved ones. Carmen Leon escaped but her father did not. "He was inside the house, and the water just carried him and everything else away," she said. "We are still looking for him, but he is probably dead, buried alive like most of the other victims." As Leon stood outside what was left of her own home she said, "Death is everywhere now. [It's] under my feet and under what is left of this place."

The mudslides shocked some people so much that they were unable to cope. They just wandered aimlessly as if in a dream. "All day and night, there were huge numbers of desperate people walking around the beach like zombies," said relief worker Jesus Rodriguez.

With mud everywhere, many people found it impossible to get clean food or drinking water. They roamed the streets looking for anything to eat or drink. Carmen Gonzalez and her twelve-year-old niece squatted on the ground next to a filthy stream. The stench of rotting garbage filled the air. "There's no water. We're going to take this water, if you can believe it," Gonzalez said. "You have to drink something. If we don't, we're going to die."

Government officials estimated that at least 10,000 people died in the mudslides. But the real number may have been much, much higher. "Any figure that we give is more in the realm of speculation than reality," said Foreign Minister Joe Rangel. "There are bodies in the sea, bodies buried under mud, bodies everywhere."

Everyone agreed that this disaster ranked among the worst in the history of Latin America. Colonel Mario Arvalaez and his soldiers played a large role in the rescue and recovery effort. As long as he kept working, he didn't have time to reflect. Only when he paused did he begin to cry. "When you stop in a moment of quiet," Arvalaez said, "you begin to feel the pain."

If you have been timed while reading this article, enter your reading time below. Then turn to the Words-per-Minute Table on page 120 and look up your reading speed (words per minute). Enter your reading speed on the graph on page 121.

Reading Time: Selection 2

_____ : _____
MINUTES   SECONDS

UNDERSTANDING IDEAS Circle the letter of the best answer.

1. **How were Joanna Saavedra and her son rescued?**

   A A helicopter arrived before the waters swept them away.

   B They were rescued by a firefighter in a boat.

   C They stayed in a tree until the waters subsided.

   D Firefighters pulled them out of the river.

2. **Which of the following was NOT caused by the heavy rains?**

   F Avalanches of mud washed away homes.

   G At least 10,000 people died in the mudslides.

   H An earthquake destroyed many villages.

   J It was impossible to get clean water.

3. **Jesus Rodriguez said that after the mudslides**

   A people were walking around like zombies

   B there were too many relief workers

   C nobody drank the water

   D everybody pitched in and went to work

4. **What happened to Colonel Arvalaez when he paused his rescue work?**

   F He decided that he had to leave the area.

   G He fell asleep.

   H He began to cry.

   J He walked around like a zombie.

SUMMARIZE For each blank, choose the word that best completes the meaning of the paragraph.

people	death	loved	
mudslides	knocked	happy	rocks

There were very few _____

stories that came out of the terrible floods in Venezuela.

The savage _____ wiped out

countless homes. More than 10,000

_____ were killed. Once the mud

started to slide, it _____ down or

covered everything in its path. It moved huge trees and

_____ the size of small cars.

Thousands of people lost their homes and

_____ ones. Carmen Leon said,

"_____ is everywhere now."

IF YOU WERE THERE Imagine you were living along the hills where the mudslides wiped out so many homes. Write a brief paragraph explaining your actions. Be sure to include examples from the story to support your response.

_____

_____

_____

_____

_____

USE CONTEXT CLUES When you read, you may find a word whose meaning is unfamiliar to you. When that happens, you can look up the word's meaning in the dictionary. You can also find out what the word means by looking for context clues. These are words or sentences that come before or after the word. Context clues can be synonyms or antonyms of the unfamiliar word. They may also be an example or definition of the unfamiliar word.

Read each excerpt from the stories you just read. Circle the letter with the best meaning of the underlined word.

1. **Rivers that were little more than a trickle quickly grew to be miles wide.**

   A thin stream

   B waterfall

   C faucet

   D tidal wave

2. **"I just wanted to be safe," she said. . . . Altogether fifteen villagers sought refuge in the same tree.**

   F safety

   G relief

   H supplies

   J options

3. **At last, on March 1, a South African helicopter arrived over the tree in Mondiano. The chopper hovered overhead as the crew began lifting people to safety.**

   A moved quickly

   B hung in the air

   C flew higher

   D landed

4. **He was also pleased by the media's coverage of the rescue. He hoped it would help everyone realize what his people had been through during this terrible flood.**

   F roof

   G protection

   H reporting

   J umbrella

5. **As long as he kept working, he didn't have time to reflect. Only when he paused did he begin to cry.**

   A shine

   B mirror

   C think about

   D throw back

PUT WORDS INTO CONTEXT Complete the paragraph using the underlined words from the exercise on this page.

Many people sought _____

from the floods in Mozambique by climbing into trees. The

river had grown from a _____

to a raging body of water. As the chopper

_____ above, the survivors had

little time to _____ about what

had happened to them. Later, news

_____ showed the entire world

how devastating the floods had been to the country.

SIMILES AND METAPHORS Writers use similes and metaphors to make their writing more vivid. Similes and metaphors are comparisons between words. Similes are easy to spot because they include the words *like* or *as*. Here's an example: *Fear sliced through her like a hot knife through butter.* Metaphors are a little different because the comparisons do not use the words *like* or *as*. Here's an example of a metaphor: *Time was their worst enemy.* In this metaphor, *time* is compared with *enemy*.

Read the following sentences. Decide whether the comparison is a simile or metaphor. Write S for simile or M for metaphor in the blank on the left.

_____ **1.** Rositha's birth was a breath of fresh air.

_____ **2.** Mud rushed through the town like water through a broken dam.

_____ **3.** People walked around like zombies

_____ **4.** The birth of Rositha was the rainbow after the storm.

_____ **5.** Mud split her house in half like an axe splits wood.

WHAT'S THE COMPARISON? Read the following sentences. In the space provided, write what two things are being compared.

1. The mud was a wrecking ball destroying houses and buildings.

_____

2. Some people were wandering as if in a dream.

_____

3. All day and night, there were people walking around like zombies.

_____

4. Roaring like a train, the mud came rushing into the shanties.

_____

PRACTICE SUMMARIZING As you now know, a summary retells the main points of a story. Summaries do not attempt to recount every detail. For example, if you look up the TV guide in a newspaper, there is often a summary of what each program is about. A sentence is usually enough to summarize a half-hour program.

Practice writing one-sentence summaries of these TV programs about disasters. Use only one sentence. You decide what the program will be about, based on the title. The first one is done for you.

TV Program and One-sentence Summary
1. "An Avalanche of Mud"
An entire town is destroyed in a terrible mudslide.
2. "Saved by a Tree"
3. "The Night the River Went Wild"
4. "The Mud That Killed a Village"

SUMMARIZE THE STORIES In the space provided, write a one-paragraph summary of each of the selections. Be sure to include only the main points from each selection.

"Miracle in a Tree"

_____

_____

_____

_____

_____

"Tragic Mudslide"

_____

_____

_____

_____

_____

_____

MAKE INFERENCES Inferences are what the reader learns from what the writer has written. When you make an inference, you consider the evidence you've read and then decide what the message is, if it has not already been clearly stated. Circle the letter of the best answer.

1. **Which of the following CANNOT be infered from the following sentences?**

> Heavy rains and a recent cyclone created the worst flood in southern Africa in more than a hundred years. No one could remember seeing Mozambique's fifteen rivers rise so fast. More than 700 people drowned and over a million were left homeless.

A Sometimes there are cyclones in southern Africa.

B There are fifteen major rivers in Mozambique.

C It would take years for Mozambique to recover.

D The rescue operation was the fastest anyone could remember.

2. **What can the reader infer about Carolina from these sentences?**

> "I was feeling a lot of pain since I spent three days without eating anything," she said. "I was hungry and thirsty and tired." Beyond that she was now in labor. But by the time the medic arrived, Carolina had already given birth to a healthy baby girl.

F Carolina gives up easily.

G Carolina needed a lot of help to have her baby.

H Carolina was not able to cope well.

J Carolina is strong and courageous.

APPLY WHAT YOU KNOW

1. **What is the author's main purpose in the first paragraph of "Miracle in a Tree"?**

A to tell the reader about Carolina's village

B to tell one person's experience of the flood

C to tell what people in Mozambique eat

D to identify types of trees in Carolina's village

2. **Read the following sentences. What impression is the author trying to give about Carmen Leon?**

> Carmen Leon escaped but her father did not. "He was inside the house, and the water just carried him and everything else away," she said. "We are still looking for him, but he is probably dead, buried alive like most of the other victims were." As Leon stood outside what was left of her own home she said, "Death is everywhere now."

F She was relieved the mudslides were over.

G She was feeling depressed and sad.

H She was feeling very hopeful.

J She was determined to find her father alive.

JUDGE THE EVIDENCE Based on what you have read from both stories, are there any similarities between the flood in Mozambique and the mudslides in Venezuela? Support your opinions with evidence from the stories you have read.

_____

_____

_____

_____

_____

_____

SELECTION 1

Icicle Baby

One-year-old Erika Nordby should have been asleep. But at about three o'clock in the morning on March 3, 2001, she wasn't. Dressed only in a T-shirt and diapers, the little girl rolled off her bed and toddled to the kitchen. She and her mother were staying at a friend's house in Edmonton, Canada. The latch on the kitchen door didn't work properly, so when a gust of wind came along, the door blew open. Little Erika wandered outside. Then the door slammed shut behind her.

Now Erika couldn't get back into the house. The ground around her was covered with a foot of snow, and the temperature was well below zero. With no protection from the elements, Erika's body temperature plummeted. Within a few minutes the little girl was frozen solid. After a while—no one was sure how long—her mother stirred and saw that Erika was missing from her bed. "I ran through the house, screaming for her, and she wasn't there," said Leyla Nordby.

Then Leyla saw the kitchen door, which the wind had blown open again. "I walked to the door," she later remembered, "and saw something lying in the snow." It was Erika, lying face down and lifeless in the snow about twenty feet from the door. "I screamed her name and ran out in my bare feet and night clothes."

When Leyla reached Erika, she was horrified by what she saw. The little girl's hair was white and thick with frost. Her mouth was frozen shut. Her eyelids looked like tiny icicles. The toddler's arms and legs were purple with frostbite. Erika's body temperature had dropped by about 50 degrees. Leyla picked her daughter up. "I scooped her up and ran inside, yelling to my friend to call for an ambulance. It was the worst feeling ever," she said. "She was stiff in my arms." Leyla wrapped the frozen girl in blankets and began to pray.

Paramedics got to the house within a few minutes. Justin Mazzolini and Krista Rempel did what they could to save Erika, but they were shocked by how cold she was. Mazzolini described how difficult it was just to touch her. "Your hands hurt like you were holding a frozen turkey," he recalled. "Her limbs were just frozen stiff like blocks of ice." He and Rempel couldn't even get a breathing tube down her throat because ice crystals blocked the way.

Erika's heart wasn't beating and she wasn't breathing, but Mazzolini and Rempel did detect signs of faint electrical activity in the girl's heart. It wasn't much to go on. Nonetheless, they kept working on Erika all the way to the hospital. "We still had to do our work," said Mazzolini later, "but I wasn't holding a lot of hope out for her. It did, at the time, seem quite hopeless."

At the University of Alberta Hospital, Erika was whisked into the emergency room. There, doctors scrambled to warm her up with heated blankets. They also planned to hook her up to a heart-lung machine. This involved redirecting her blood through a device where the blood would be heated, so that warmed blood could be returned to her body. But before doctors had the machine in place, Erika's heart started beating again *on its own*. Her blood had warmed up enough by itself so that she didn't need the machine. The hospital staff was stunned by this miraculous turn of events.

When Leyla heard the good news, she couldn't believe it. "I was overjoyed," she said, "but I didn't understand it because five hours before, she was dead. I never believed in miracles, but my little girl is living proof that they can happen."

Doctor Allen De Caen couldn't quite believe it, either. He said, "When Erika arrived, her heart had been stopped for at least two hours. By every textbook definition, she was dead. But we didn't give up." He went on to say that Erika's heart "just started to beat on its own. It was a miracle."

The girl's size helped. Erika was so small that her body froze very quickly.

When her heart and lungs stopped working, her brain stopped receiving oxygen. Ordinarily, that would have resulted in brain damage. But Erika's body temperature dropped so fast that her entire system shut down before damage occurred.

Doctors worried that Erika might lose some toes to frostbite. But by using skin grafts from her thigh, they were able to save all her toes. The only long-term physical disability Erika suffered was that her left foot didn't grow as long as her right. Luckily, she could easily compensate for that by wearing a special shoe.

Erika Nordby's story made headlines around the world. Letters, postcards, and prayers from total strangers flooded into the hospital. One five-year-old girl sent her own sweater, saying she didn't want "the baby to be cold again." Many people called Erika the "Ice Baby" or the "Human Popsicle." But to the hospital staff, Erika Nordby would always be remembered by the nickname they gave her on the morning of March 3, 2001: "Miracle."

If you have been timed while reading this article, enter your reading time below. Then turn to the Words-per-Minute Table on page 120 and look up your reading speed (words per minute). Enter your reading speed on the graph on page 121.

Reading Time: Selection 1

_____ : _____
MINUTES   SECONDS

UNDERSTANDING IDEAS Circle the letter of the best answer.

1. How did Erika Nordby end up in the snow?

 A She fell asleep outside.

 B She fell out of a window.

 C She walked through the open kitchen door.

 D She kept slipping on the ice.

2. After Leyla noticed that Erika was gone, she ran through the house, and

 F noticed that the kitchen door was open

 G found her daughter in the kitchen

 H found her daughter in the basement

 J woke up her friend to ask her for help

3. Which of the following statements is FALSE?

 A Erika was frozen solid.

 B The paramedics never gave up on her.

 C Doctors heated her with warm blankets.

 D Erika never recovered from her ordeal.

4. The doctors were able to save Erika's toes by

 F using skin grafts from her thigh

 G making sure that they were heated quickly

 H giving her special shoes to wear

 J using a new radiation technique

SUMMARIZE For each blank, choose the word that best completes the meaning of the paragraph.

| small | paramedics | |
| icy | lying | heart |

Erika Nordby was only one year old when she walked out into the _____ night of March 3, 2001. She quickly froze solid and her mother found her _____ in the snow. When the _____ arrived, her heart was not beating and she was not breathing. Miraculously, as the doctors at the hospital began to warm her up, her _____ began beating on its own. The doctors thought that she lived because she was so _____ .

IF YOU WERE THERE What would you do if you found a very small child frozen in the snow? Write a brief paragraph explaining your actions. Be sure to include examples from the story in your response.

_____
_____
_____
_____
_____

No Way Out

Doug Custer was about to call it quits. It was nine o'clock in the evening on Wednesday, July 24, 2002, and Custer was nearing the end of his shift in the Quecreek Mine in Somerset, Pennsylvania.

"All of a sudden, a call came in on the walkie-talkie," Custer later recalled. It came from a group of nine other miners in a nearby section of the mine. "They said, 'We hit water—get out!' In a mine we joke around a lot, but we know a call like this is serious." Custer and the seven men with him dropped their tools, turned off their machinery, and raced up out of the mine. They barely made it. Water was gushing into the tunnel all around them. "Pretty soon it was a serious current running hard against our legs," said Custer.

After reaching safety, Custer looked around for the men who had sounded the alarm. "My first thought was, 'Where are the other guys? Did they get out?'"

They hadn't. Those nine miners were trapped 240 feet below the surface. They had struck a huge underground pocket of water that wasn't accurately labeled on any map. When they hit it, more than 50 million gallons of water began pouring into the mine. John Unger, one of the nine miners, later described this massive flow of water. "I've never seen anything with so much rage in my entire

life," he said. "There was no way out."

After signaling Custer's crew on the walkie-talkie, the nine miners ran for their lives. The water swirled around their waists, their shoulders, their necks. Frantically they searched for higher ground, but the water kept coming.

"I said to myself, 'This is it,'" recalled Harry Mayhugh.

"Death was staring me in the face," said Ron Hileman, "and it was coming to get me."

Finally the men did find a relatively dry place. But they were trapped deep underground with no idea when—or if—rescuers would find them. From the beginning they pledged to work together, deciding to live or die as a unit. So when one of them found a lunch box in the tunnel, they divided its contents— a corned-beef sandwich and bottle of water—into nine equal portions. They huddled together to share body heat and worked constantly to buoy each other's spirits. "When somebody would get low, we'd all work to cheer them up," explained Mayhugh. "Then you'd be down, and everybody worked on you."

Meanwhile, rescue workers were struggling to locate the nine miners. Mining expert Joseph Shaffoni knew approximately where the men had been when they hit water. From there he figured they headed for the highest ground. After surveying diagrams of the mine's various tunnels, he selected a spot and told rescuers to begin digging. "You do the survey," Shaffoni said, "you come close, but then it's by guess and by God where they are."

Fortunately, his guess was a good one. When drillers managed to punch a six-inch air pipe down into the tunnel, the trapped miners saw it immediately. They tapped nine times on the pipe to indicate that all nine of them were still alive. The sounds of their tapping gave the rescuers a tremendous boost. Even so, rescue crews knew they were a long way from getting the men out. They began a desperate, round-the-clock effort to carve a 30-inch-wide escape hole down to the tunnel.

The miners waited by the air pipe as long as they could, but eventually the water began rising around them again and they were forced to move away. When their tapping stopped, the people up above feared the worst. Nonetheless, rescuers continued to dig, drill, and pray.

As the hours passed, the miners faced the possibility that help might not arrive in time. At about 2:00 A.M. on Friday, the rescue effort hit a heartrending snag. A 1500-pound drill bit broke, forcing rescuers to shut down the drill for eighteen hours while repairmen worked on it. When the trapped miners heard the sudden silence, they didn't know what to think. They prayed that the rescue effort hadn't been called off.

By eight o'clock Friday night, the drill was working again. For the next twenty-six hours, rescuers drilled farther and farther into the earth. At 10:16 P.M. on Saturday, they finally broke through the ceiling of the tunnel. By then, the miners

had been trapped for seventy-three hours and there had been no communication with them in more than two days. No one wanted to ask the question, but everyone was wondering the same thing: were the men still alive?

Within seconds, that question was answered. From down in the mine came tapping on the air pipe. It was an incredible moment. "I just can't tell you what that was like," said driller John Hamilton.

Rescuers dropped a telephone down into the hole and Ray McKinney, a mine safety official, spoke into the receiver, calling out, "Anybody there?"

"Yes," joked a voice on the other end, "what took you so long?"

When rescuers realized that all nine men were alive and in relatively good shape, a wave of joy swept over them. And when all nine were finally pulled to safety at 2:45 A.M., the celebration began. One of the greatest mine rescues of all time had been successfully completed.

If you have been timed while reading this article, enter your reading time below. Then turn to the Words-per-Minute Table on page 120 and look up your reading speed (words per minute). Enter your reading speed on the graph on page 121.

Reading Time: Selection 2

_____ : _____
MINUTES   SECONDS

UNDERSTANDING IDEAS Circle the letter of the best answer.

1. **What did the nine miners tell Doug Custer over the walkie-talkie?**

   A There's been an explosion.

   B Part of the tunnel has caved in.

   C We've hit water—get out!

   D It's time to quit work and go home.

2. **What did Custer discover after he reached safety?**

   F The nine miners had not made it out.

   G The nine miners were waiting for them outside.

   H Three miners were trapped in the mine.

   J They could go back to work.

3. **What conclusion can the reader draw from the following comment?**

   > "I said to myself, 'This is it.'"

   A He felt safe.

   B He found something he had lost.

   C He figured out how to stop the water.

   D He thought he was going to die.

4. **How would you describe the relationships between the nine miners?**

   F cooperative

   G angry

   H weak

   J judgmental

SUMMARIZE For each blank, choose the word that best completes the meaning of the paragraph.

water	dry	survived
miners	group	higher

Nine _____ were trapped 240 feet under the ground in Somerset, Pennsylvania. They had struck _____, and more than 50 million gallons poured into the mine. They ran for their lives and tried to find _____ ground. Finally, they found a place where they were relatively _____. They agreed that they would live or die as a _____. This had a lot to do with why they _____.

IF YOU WERE THERE What would you do if you were trapped in a mine? Write a brief paragraph explaining your actions. Be sure to include examples from the story to support your response.

_____

_____

_____

_____

_____

_____

_____

USE CONTEXT CLUES When you read, you may find a word whose meaning is unfamiliar to you. When that happens, you can look up the word's meaning in the dictionary. You can also find out what the word means by looking for context clues. These are words or sentences that come before or after the word. Context clues can be synonyms or antonyms of the unfamiliar word. They may also be an example or definition of the unfamiliar word.

Read each excerpt from the stories you just read. Circle the letter with the best meaning of the underlined word.

1. **The ground around her was covered with a foot of snow and the temperature was well below zero. With no protection from the elements, Erika's body temperature <u>plummeted</u>.**

   A rose

   B fell quickly

   C dropped slowly

   D increased rapidly

2. **At the University of Alberta Hospital, Erika was <u>whisked</u> into the emergency room. Doctors scrambled to warm her up with heated blankets.**

   F moved quickly

   G moved slowly

   H brushed

   J swept clean

3. **The only long-term physical disability Erika suffered was that her left foot didn't grow as long as her right. Luckily, she could easily <u>compensate</u> for that by wearing a special shoe.**

   A make up for

   B move around

   C take away from

   D get even for

4. **From the beginning they <u>pledged</u> to work together, deciding to live or die as a unit. So when one of them found a lunch box in the tunnel, they divided its contents—a corned-beef sandwich and bottle of water—into nine equal portions.**

   F refused

   G disagreed

   H were able

   J promised

5. **They huddled together to share body heat and worked constantly to <u>buoy</u> each other's spirits.**

   A keep up

   B signal

   C lower

   D sink

PUT WORDS INTO CONTEXT Complete the paragraph using the underlined words from the exercise on this page.

When Erika Norby was found frozen

in the snow, her mother called the paramedics who

_____ Erika to the hospital. To

_____ for her low body

temperature, the doctors warmed her with heated

blankets. They _____ to do all

they could to help Erika. Her mother's spirits had

_____ since finding her

daughter's lifeless body, but when Erika's heart started

beating again, her spirits soared.

MAKE ROOT CONNECTIONS One way of finding out the meaning of a word is by looking for its root. An unfamiliar word may share a common root with a word that you know. A root is a part of many different words and may not be a word by itself. The root *aster* or *astro* comes from a Greek word that means "star." You will find the root in words like *asteroid* and *astronomy*.

Underline the root that connects each group of words. Then choose the best meaning of the root.

1. **document, docudrama, documentary**
   - **A** based on real events
   - **B** roles taken by actors
   - **C** made of paper and ink
   - **D** stories made from imagination

2. **predict, indicate, verdict**
   - **F** to lie
   - **G** to say
   - **H** to recall
   - **J** to foresee

3. **biology, biofeedback, biography**
   - **A** about traveling
   - **B** about life
   - **C** about sight
   - **D** about hearing

4. **investigate, vestige, investigator**
   - **F** track or trace
   - **G** look and see
   - **H** hint or tell
   - **J** invest or earn

5. **prescribe, describe, inscribe**
   - **A** to walk
   - **B** to listen
   - **C** to write
   - **D** to see

6. **territory, extraterrestrial, terrain**
   - **F** ocean, sea
   - **G** earth, land
   - **H** sky, air
   - **J** sun, light

ROOT ANALOGIES Analogies show similar patterns and relationships between words. Root analogies show relationships between words that have the same root word. For example, *use* is to *useable* as *move* is to *moveable*. Both root words, when combined with *able*, make a new word. For each blank, choose one of the boldfaced words on this page to correctly complete the analogy.

1. *moment* is to *momentary* as *document* is to

   _____ .

2. *a* is to *ascribe* as *pre* is to

   _____ .

3. *photo* is to *photography* as *bio* is to

   _____ .

4. *orna* is to *ornament* as *docu* is to

   _____ .

ORGANIZE IDEAS Let's review. The main ideas in a story are the main topics that are discussed. The specific details are the facts that clarify or support the main ideas. Fill in the chart by using the items listed at the right. If the bulleted item is a main idea from the story, write it in the row marked "Main Idea." If the item is a detail that supports the main idea, write it in the row marked "Detail."

"Icicle Baby"
Main Idea:
Detail:
Detail:
Detail:
Detail:

"No Way Out"
Main Idea:
Detail:
Detail:
Detail:
Detail:

- Erika's body froze quickly.

- The miners tapped on the air pipe.

- Erika's mother found her and called paramedics.

- Erika Nordby was frozen and brought back to life.

- Rescuers drilled a 30-inch-wide hole.

- In the summer of 2002, nine miners got trapped 240 feet under the ground.

- Rescue workers punched a 6-inch air pipe down into the tunnel.

- Doctors warmed up Erika and her heart began to beat.

- The nine miners vowed to work together to survive.

- Erika walked outside and could not get back into the house.

SUPPORT THE MAIN IDEA Write a paragraph about the possibility of someone surviving an accident against the odds. State the main idea in the first sentence. Then use details from both stories to support your main idea.

_____

_____

_____

_____

_____

_____

_____

VERIFYING EVIDENCE Because misinformation gets printed sometimes, you must verify the accuracy of everything you read. The way to do that is to weigh the evidence presented and decide whether it is trustworthy. Sometimes part of an article may present the correct facts about something, and part of the same article may mislead you. You have to decide whether to believe all or only parts of the information you've read.

Read the following sentences taken from "No Way Out." Choose the best answer for each question.

[1] "I said to myself, 'This is it,'" recalled Harry Mayhugh. [2] "Death was staring me in the face," agreed Ron Hileman, "and it was coming to get me." [3] The men were trapped deep underground with no idea when—or if—rescuers would find them. [4] No one wanted to ask the question, but everyone was wondering the same thing: were the men still alive? [5] When all nine men were finally pulled to safety, the celebration began.

1. **What evidence would best support Mayhugh's feeling that he might die?**

   A Doug Custer and the other men escaped.

   B The men had no idea if they would be rescued.

   C The men found a dry place.

   D Rescuers were doing everything they could.

2. **Which sentence in the paragraph would be most difficult to verify?**

   F Sentence 2

   G Sentence 3

   H Sentence 4

   J Sentence 5

3. **Which sentence suggests that more than one rescuer thought the miners might die?**

   A Sentence 1

   B Sentence 2

   C Sentence 3

   D Sentence 4

JUDGE THE EVIDENCE To persuade the reader of an opinion, the author often provides evidence. It is up to the reader to judge if the evidence presented is believable or not.

1. **Which of the following is evidence that the miners worked together to survive?**

   A They found higher ground above the water.

   B They shared a corn beef sandwich nine ways.

   C They tapped on the air pipe.

   D They were trapped 240 feet below the surface.

2. **Which statement is evidence the miners thought they might die?**

   F "Death was staring me in the face," said Ron Hileman.

   G The drill bit had to be repaired.

   H The miners tapped nine times on the air pipe.

   J Workers struggled to locate the miners.

PERSUADE WITH EVIDENCE Write two sentences persuading your reader that no matter how bad a situation may appear, you should keep trying to rescue or revive someone. Be sure to include examples from the stories to support your answer.

_____

_____

_____

_____

Words-per-Minute Table

If you were timed while reading, find your reading time in the column on the left. Find the unit and number of the story across the top of the chart. Follow the time row across to its intersection with the column of the story. This is your reading speed. Go to the next page to plot your progress.

Unit →	1	1	2	2	3	3	4	4	5	5	6	6	7	7	8	8	9	9	10	10
Selection → Time ↓	1	2	1	2	1	2	1	2	1	2	1	2	1	2	1	2	1	2	1	2
1:20	874	797	907	900	889	875	787	877	907	938	854	880	915	908	882	796	750	766	849	886
1:40	539	598	719	675	667	656	590	658	701	704	646	660	686	681	702	597	563	575	637	693
2:00	450	478	575	540	533	525	472	526	561	563	516	528	549	545	561	478	450	460	509	554
2:20	385	399	480	450	445	438	394	439	468	469	431	440	458	454	468	398	375	383	425	462
2:40	337	342	411	386	381	375	337	376	401	402	369	377	392	389	401	341	321	328	364	396
3:00	300	299	360	337	333	328	295	329	351	352	323	330	343	340	351	298	281	287	318	346
3:20	270	266	320	300	296	292	262	292	312	313	287	293	305	303	312	265	250	255	283	308
3:40	245	239	288	270	267	263	236	263	281	281	258	264	275	272	281	239	225	230	255	277
4:00	225	217	262	245	242	239	215	239	255	256	235	240	250	248	255	217	205	209	232	252
4:20	207	199	240	225	222	219	197	219	234	235	215	220	229	227	234	199	188	192	212	231
4:40	193	184	221	208	205	202	182	202	216	216	199	203	211	210	216	184	173	177	196	213
5:00	180	171	205	193	190	187	169	188	200	201	184	189	196	195	201	171	161	164	182	198
5:20	169	159	192	180	178	175	157	175	187	188	172	176	183	182	187	159	150	153	170	185
5:40	159	149	180	169	167	164	148	164	175	176	161	165	172	170	176	149	141	144	159	173
6:00	150	141	169	159	157	154	139	155	165	166	152	155	161	160	165	140	132	135	150	163
6:20	142	133	160	150	148	146	131	146	156	156	144	147	153	151	156	133	125	128	142	154
6:40	135	126	151	142	140	138	124	138	148	148	136	139	144	143	148	126	118	121	134	146
7:00	128	120	144	135	133	131	118	132	140	141	129	132	137	136	140	119	112	115	127	139
7:20	123	114	137	129	127	125	112	125	134	134	123	126	131	130	134	114	107	109	121	132
7:40	117	109	131	123	121	119	107	120	128	128	117	120	125	124	128	109	102	104	116	126
8:00	112	104	125	117	116	114	103	114	122	122	112	115	119	118	122	104	98	100	111	121
8:20	108	100	120	113	111	109	98	110	117	117	108	110	114	114	117	100	94	96	106	116
8:40	104	96	115	108	107	105	94	105	112	113	103	106	110	109	112	96	90	92	102	111
9:00	100	92	111	104	103	101	91	101	108	108	99	102	106	105	108	92	87	88	98	107
9:20	96	89	107	100	99	97	87	97	104	104	96	98	102	101	104	88	83	85	94	103
9:40	93	85	103	96	95	94	84	94	100	101	92	94	98	97	100	85	80	82	91	99
10:00	90	82	99	93	92	91	81	91	97	97	89	91	95	94	97	82	78	79	88	96
10:20	87	80	96	90	89	88	79	88	94	94	86	88	92	91	94	80	75	77	85	92
10:40	84	77	93	87	86	85	76	85	90	91	83	85	89	88	91	77	73	74	82	89
11:00	82	75	90	84	83	82	74	82	88	88	81	82	86	85	88	75	70	72	80	87
11:20	79	72	87	82	81	80	72	80	85	85	78	80	83	83	85	72	68	70	77	84
11:40	77	70	85	79	78	77	69	77	83	83	76	78	81	80	83	70	66	68	75	82
12:00	75	68	82	77	76	75	67	75	80	80	74	75	78	78	80	68	64	66	73	79
12:20	73	66	80	75	74	73	66	73	78	78	72	73	76	76	78	66	63	64	71	77
12:40	71	65	78	73	72	71	64	71	76	76	70	71	74	74	76	65	61	62	69	75
13:00	69	63	76	71	70	69	62	69	74	74	68	69	72	72	74	63	59	60	67	73
13:20	67	61	74	69	68	67	61	67	72	72	66	68	70	70	72	61	58	59	65	71
13:40	66	60	72	68	67	66	59	66	70	70	65	66	69	68	70	60	56	57	64	69
14:00	64	58	70	66	65	64	58	64	68	69	63	64	67	66	68	58	55	56	62	68
14:20	63	57	67	64	64	63	56	63	67	65	62	63	65	65	67	57	54	55	61	66
14:40	61	54	65	62	62	60	54	60	64	64	60	61	62	63	65	54	52	53	59	64
15:00	60	53	64	60	59	58	52	58	62	63	57	59	61	61	62	53	50	51	57	62

Plotting Your Progress: Reading Speed

Enter your words-per-minute rate in the box above the appropriate lesson. Then place a small X on the line directly above the number of the lesson, across from the number of words per minute you read. Graph your progress by drawing a line to connect the X's.

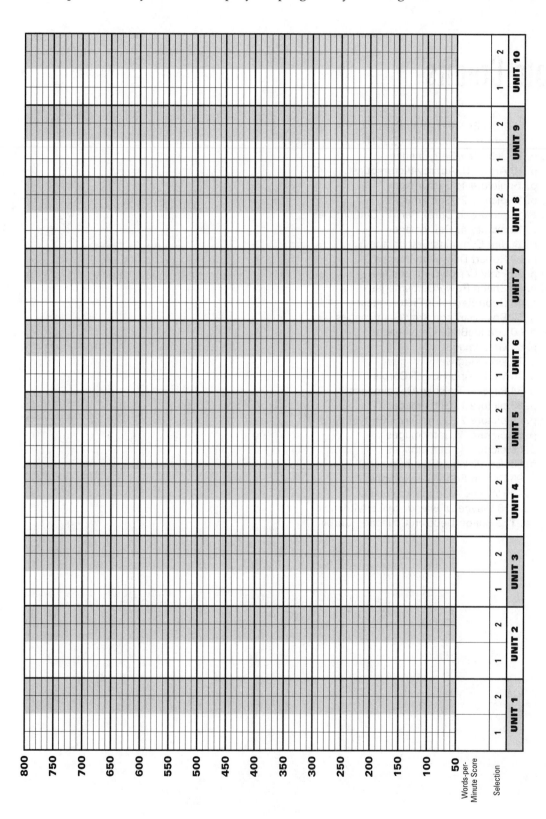

Photo Credits

Unit 1: p. vi Brian Bailey/Gettyimages
Unit 1: p. 3 picture 1: Robert Van Der Hilst/Gettyimages
Unit 2: p. 12 Julie Toy/Gettyimages
Unit 2: p. 16 Arthur S. Aubrey/Picturequest
Unit 2: p. 19 picture 1: Gettyimages
Unit 2: p. 19 picture 2: Gettyimages
Unit 2: p. 19 picture 3: Derek Berwin/Gettyimages
Unit 2: p. 19 picture 4: Gettyimages
Unit 3: p. 24 Jim Cummins/Gettyimages
Unit 3: p. 28 Robert Daly/Gettyimages
Unit 4: p. 36 Patty Carroll/Gettyimages
Unit 4: p. 40 Shahn Rowe/Gettyimages
Unit 5: p. 48 Deon Reynolds/Picturequest
Unit 5: p. 52 Ross Harrison Koty/Gettyimages
Unit 6: p. 60 Joe McBride/Gettyimages
Unit 6: p. 64 Gettyimages
Unit 7: p. 72 Don King/Gettyimages
Unit 7: p. 76 V.C.L./Tipp Howell/Corbis
Unit 8: p. 84 Pascale Treichler/Gettyimages
Unit 8: p. 86 picture 1: Gettyimages
Unit 8: p. 86 picture 2: Sami Sarkis/Gettyimages
Unit 8: p. 86 picture 3: Gettyimages
Unit 8: p. 86 picture 4: Gettyimages
Unit 8: p. 88 Jim Pickerell/Picturequest
Unit 9: p. 96 Darren Robb/Gettyimages
Unit 9: p. 100 Wayne Aldridge/Imagestate
Unit 10: p. 108 Wayne D. Bilenduke/Gettyimages
Unit 10: p. 112 Hulton-Deutsch Collection/Corbis